RAMESES III
KING OF EGYPT

RAMESES III
KING OF EGYPT

HIS LIFE AND AFTERLIFE

AIDAN DODSON

The American University in Cairo Press
Cairo   New York

First published in 2019 by
The American University in Cairo Press
113 Sharia Kasr el Aini, Cairo, Egypt
200 Park Ave., Suite 1700, New York, NY 10166

Dar el Kutub No. 3526/19
ISBN 978 977 416 940 3

Dar el Kutub Cataloging-in-Publication Data

Dodson, Aidan
        Rameses III, King of Egypt: His Life and Afterlife / Aidan Dodson.—Cairo: The American University in Cairo Press, 2019.
                p.   cm.
                ISBN: 978 977 416 940 3
                1-   Ramses III, King of Egypt
                2-   Egypt— History — To 332 B.C.
                3-   Pharaohs — Biography
                932.014092

1 2 3 4 5   23 22 21 20 19

Designed by Sally Boylan
Printed in China

In memory of Sheila Mary Hilton
(1934–2019)

CONTENTS

PREFACE

This book represents the second (following on from my recent volume on Sethy I) in a series that aims to provide accounts of key figures of ancient Egyptian history, covering not only their life story but also their rediscovery and reception in modern times. The present subject, Rameses III, has often been called the 'last great pharaoh,' but although his key monuments have been the subject of comprehensive publication,[1] he has been poorly served by dedicated monographs on his reign as a whole. An excellent overview exists in French,[2] but the principal book in English[3] suffers from being an edited work, not only made up of contributions of variable quality, but also often lacking focus on the third Rameses, with much of its force dissipated in issues concerning the broader Ramesside Period.

It is against this background that the present work is offered to Egyptological professionals, students, and enthusiasts, providing a fully documented and extensively illustrated summary of what we know about Rameses III, his time, and monuments, and also the way in which his monuments—and even his physical body—emerged from obscurity to be the subject of research over the past four centuries. In aiming to address such a wide audience, there have had to be a number of compromises as to depth and breadth of focus, but it is hoped that such compromises have not been too gross, and that a balanced picture of the state of research, and in particular enduring areas of debate, has been provided.

Thanks go to various friends and colleagues for their help in writing this book and in the provision of images, in particular Florence Barbiero, Leslie D. Black, Peter A. Clayton, Steve Cross, Martin Davies, Peter James, Sara Orel, David Robbins, and Anke Weber. In addition, my wife, Dyan Hilton, is to be thanked for continuing to put up with me, as well as taking a number of photographs used in this book and proofreading the manuscript alongside Victoria Baylis-Jones and Reg Clarke. All residual errors and faulty reasoning remain, of course, my own fault!

ABBREVIATIONS AND CONVENTIONS

BibNat	Bibliothèque Nationale, Paris, France.
BM	British Museum, London, UK.
Brooklyn	Brooklyn Museum, New York, USA.
Cairo	Egyptian Museum, Cairo, Egypt.
Durham	Oriental Museum, University of Durham, UK.
Fitzwilliam	Fitzwilliam Museum, Cambridge, UK.
Florence	Museo Archeologico, Florence, Italy.
Liverpool	National Museums Liverpool, UK.
Louvre	Musée du Louvre, Paris, France.
LPH	Life, Prosperity, and Health (ancient wish).
o	Ostracon (number/name).
oDM	Deir el-Medina ostracon.
OIM	Oriental Institute Museum, University of Chicago, USA.
p	Papyrus (number/name)
Petrie	Petrie Museum, University College, London, UK.
PML	Pierpoint Morgan Library, New York, USA.
Rockefeller	Rockefeller Museum, East Jerusalem, Israel.
Stockholm	Medelhavsmuseet, Stockholm, Sweden.
Turin	Museo Egizio, Turin, Italy.
UPMAA	University of Pennsylvania Museum of Archaeology & Anthropology, Philadelphia, USA.

INTRODUCTION

Rameses III lived and ruled during a pivotal epoch in the history of the eastern Mediterranean. By the early twelfth century BC, the region had experienced some three centuries of exceptional prosperity. Although by no means without conflict, both between major states and against 'rebellious' vassals, there had been broad stability between a set of mutually recognized 'great powers.' These entities corresponded with one another, enjoyed formal diplomatic relationships, and entered into political intermarriage—although, while happy to wed foreign princesses, the Egyptian pharaohs always demurred at offering their own daughters in the international diplomatic marriage market.

However, pressures were now building up outside this golden circle of Egypt, Palestine, Mesopotamia, and the Hittite Empire, and may have been an impetus toward the treaty of peace and friendship agreed between the Egyptians and Hittites in the middle of the thirteenth century, after some decades of warfare. 'Non-state' actors from the Aegean and beyond, in the northwest, combined with others from Libya to upset the status quo, culminating in what has been termed the 'Bronze Age Collapse' that left the region all but unrecognizable by the end of the twelfth century.

Rameses played an important role in these events, with the result that Egypt remained the only Late Bronze Age state bordering the eastern Mediterranean that continued,

FIGURE 1 Granite statue of Rameses III; from Karnak, but its original location in the temple is unknown as it was found in the great Ptolemaic statuary deposit in the Cour de la cachette (Cairo CG42150).

superficially intact, into the following centuries. But alongside the glow of his military victories, his reign also witnessed internal economic and political decay, culminating in the king's assassination, led by members of his own household. While the dynasty survived for the time being, half a century later the country had split between north and south and was riven by civil strife, out of which it emerged greatly enfeebled, a state from which it would not recover for over a century and a half.

1 FROM CRADLE TO THRONE

The future Rameses III was probably born around the end of the sixty-seven-year reign of Rameses II.[1] He was the son of one Sethnakhte, later the founder of the Twentieth Dynasty, but of unknown origin, although we know that his mother was a certain Tiye (B),[2] who added the cognomen Mereniset to her name when her husband became king (fig. 2). The name of another apparent queen of Sethnakhte, Sitre-[ta]meri, is mentioned in Sethnakhte's tomb (page 14, below), but nothing else is known of her.

The fact that Sethnakhte would later feel himself able to challenge for the throne and his name's incorporation of that of the god Seth, clearly regarded by the kings of the Nineteenth Dynasty as their patron,[3] would strongly suggest that he was a scion of that royal line. Rameses II had around a hundred children, and many left descendants, including at least two of his first three heirs apparent (Amenhirkopeshef A, Rameses B, and Khaemwaset C), whose premature deaths deprived not only them, but also their descendants, of the throne. Unlike in many other monarchies, in Egypt a defunct heir's rights did not automatically devolve on his own children: the throne went to the eldest living son at the time of the elder king's death, and then on to his descendants.

Thus, Rameses II was followed on the throne by his thirteenth son, Merenptah, although sons of a late elder brother and former heir apparent, Khaemwaset C, were certainly alive at the time. That their exclusion was by no means a slight on them is indicated by the fact that one, Hori (A), had followed his father as high priest at Memphis, and his own son and namesake, Hori (I), would soon become vizier and serve as such for some three decades (see page 8, 50, below). That Sethnakhte might have been a son or grandson of another of the elder sons seems not unlikely, and could explain why he felt himself a potential pharaoh following the extinction of the line of Merenptah at the end of the Nineteenth Dynasty.[4]

FIGURE 2 Stela of Meresyotef, *w'b*-priest of Userkhaure-meryamun (Sethnakhte), with Rameses III offering to Osiris, Horus, and Isis in the upper register, and the owner to Sethnakhte and the King's Great Wife and King's Mother Tiye-mereniset in the lower one; from Abydos (Cairo JE20395).

This came at the end of a decade-and-a-half's conflict within the royal family, which had begun soon after the death of Merenptah, when his son and successor Sethy II had been challenged by a rival king Amenmeses, possibly Sethy's own younger son. The rebellion seems to have begun in Nubia, where Amenmeses appears previously to have served as viceroy, under the name Messuy, the usurper obtaining control of much of the Nile Valley, perhaps as far north as the Fayyum. Amenmeses certainly controlled Thebes, constructing his tomb there and making additions to a number of temples. It was only after four years that Sethy II regained control of the south, presumably having defeated Amenmeses. In the interim, he presumably based himself at Per-Rameses (modern Qantir), the royal-residence city in the northeast Delta founded at the beginning of the dynasty.

However, Sethy died a little over a year later, to be followed by a young boy named Siptah, under the tutelage of the dowager queen Tawosret and the chancellor Bay, a man of possible Syrian heritage. Siptah may have been a son of the late Amenmeses, and Bay makes explicit his exceptional role as a 'king-maker' in a number of inscriptions. Bay's extraordinary status is made concrete by his possession of a tomb (KV13) of kingly proportions in the Valley of the Kings, cut next to that of Tawosret (KV14), a monument of very similar design and original decoration. Their possession of apparent 'his-and-hers' tombs recalls the 'his-and-hers' sarcophagi of the Eighteenth Dynasty female king Hatshepsut and her close associate Senenmut,[5] and leads to similar suspicions as to the nature of their personal relationship. However, whatever association there was between the chancellor and the dowager queen came to an abrupt end with the execution of Bay in Year 5 of Siptah—on the command of "Pharaoh," but most probably at the instigation of Tawosret, rather than the teenage monarch himself.

A year later, Siptah was himself dead, his names excised from the walls of his tomb, and Tawosret a fully-fledged female king, continuing Siptah's year-count. It seems likely to have been the death of Siptah that triggered Sethnakhte's rebellion, and from which point he subsequently counted his regnal years. Its successful outcome is described in a victory stela that Sethnakhte erected on the island of Elephantine at Aswan (fig. 3):

FIGURE 3 The victory stela of Sethnakhte; from Elephantine (Elephantine Museum Annex).

> The great assembly of the gods is pleased with his plans like Re, since the land had been in confusion . . . . [The great god] stretched out his arm and selected his person, LPH, from among the millions, dismissing the hundreds of thousands prior to him . . . .
>
> Now his person, LPH, was like his father Sutekh, who flexed his arms to rid Egypt of those who had led it astray . . . . Fear of him has seized the hearts of opponents before him: they flee like [flocks] of sparrows with a falcon after them. They left silver and gold . . . which they had given to these Asiatics in order for them

to bring reinforcements . . . . Their plans failed and the plans were futile, as every god and goddess performed wonders for the good god, proclaiming the [onse]t of a slaughter under him . . . .

On Year 2, II *šmw* 10 there were no (more) opponents of his person, LPH, in any lands. They came to inform his person, LPH: 'Let your heart be happy, O lord of this land; those things that the god foretold have come to pass and your foes do not exist in the land . . . .'[6]

Here, Sethnakhte claims the throne through divine selection, as the gods' means of rescuing Egypt from chaos. Further, the country's parlous state is blamed on those who had "led it astray" and had attempted to defend themselves from Sethnakhte's onslaught by trying to hire in mercenaries from Syria–Palestine.

A complementary picture of Sethnakhte's acquisition of the throne is contained in the Great Harris Papyrus (pHarris I), a memorial document produced following the death of Rameses III (see pages 79–81), and including an 'historical' section looking back over his career and the way in which his dynasty came to be founded (fig. 4):

The land of Egypt had been banished, every man being a law unto himself; they had had no leader for many years previously until other times when the land of Egypt was in the hands of chieftains and mayors; one killed his neighbor, whether high or low. Then another time came consisting of empty years when Irsu, a Syrian, was among them as a chieftain, having made the whole land into subjection before him; each joined with his companion in plundering their goods, and they treated the gods as they did men, and no offerings were made in the temples. But the gods then inclined themselves to peace so as to put the land in its proper state in accordance with its normal condition, and they established their son, who came forth from their flesh, as ruler of every land, upon their great throne, Userkhaure-setpenre-meryamun, Son of Re Sethnakhte-mererre-meryamun. He was Khepri-Seth when he was enraged; he set in order the entire land that had been rebellious; he killed the rebels who were in the land of Egypt. He cleansed the great throne of Egypt, being the ruler of the Two Lands on the throne of Atum.[7]

Such a lurid depiction of a benighted Egypt awaiting its savior is a common motif in Egyptian royal literature, examples produced in the recent past having been the Restoration Stela of Tutankhamun, marking the definitive return to orthodoxy after the 'heresy' of Akhenaten, and the Edict of Horemheb, remedying corruption within the state.[8]

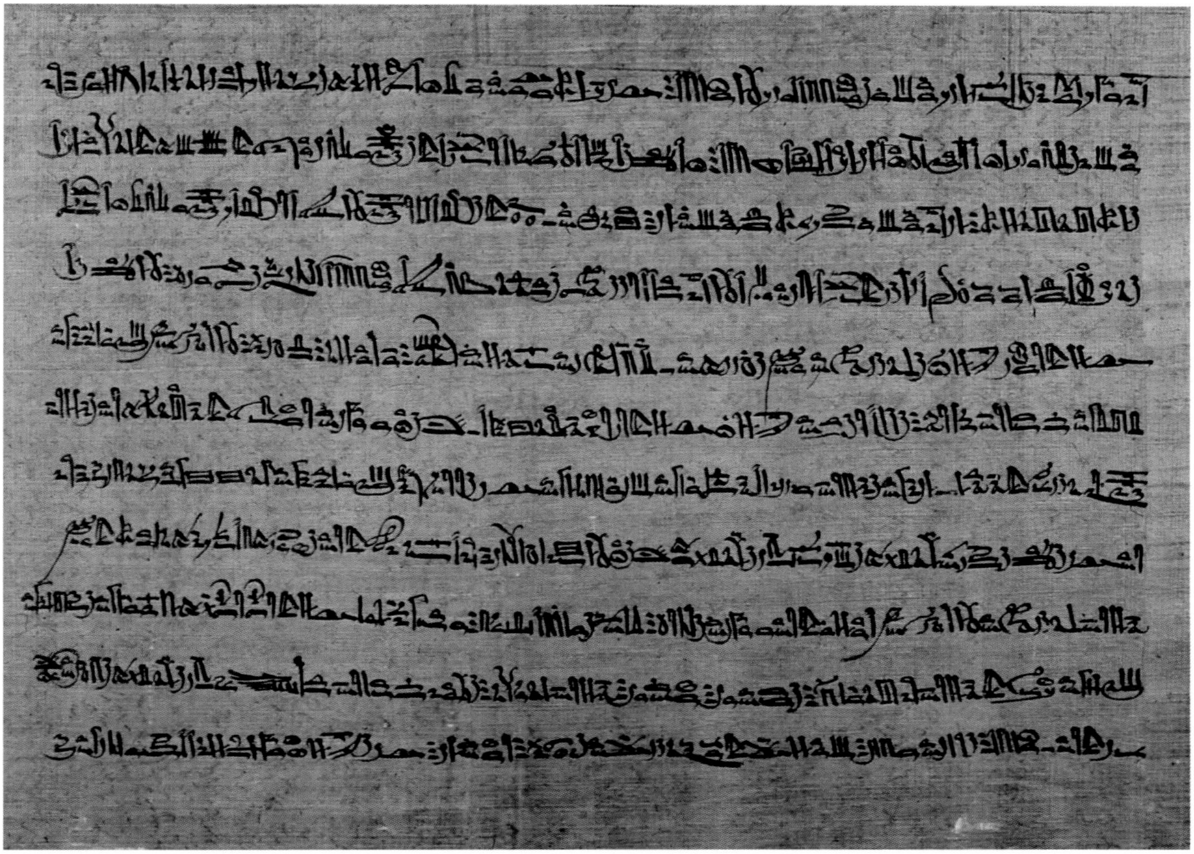

FIGURE 4 The 'historical' section of the Great Harris Papyrus; from Thebes (British Museum pEA9999,76).

The propagandistic intent of both the stela and the papyrus is thus clear, with the result that neither can be regarded uncritically as sources for the precise state of Egypt at the time Sethnakhte appeared on the scene. The papyrus also suffers from having been written more than three decades after the events in question. On the other hand, it is unlikely that events were wholly falsified, and "Irsu" has frequently been equated with the chancellor Bay. The extreme hostility expressed toward the "Syrian" and the dismissal of the time of his ascendancy as "empty years" would suggest approval for the chancellor's execution, and the possible presence of Sethnakhte at the court of Siptah and Tawosret at that time.

Sethnakhte adopted a titulary that hearkened back to that of Sethy II, actually copying his main Horus name. His two variant Golden Falcon names ("Powerful of arm who drives out his rebels" and "He who smites the Nine Bows who oppose the kingship") would seem to allude to the means by which the new king came to the throne. His reign following his victory was long regarded as having been extremely brief, but in 2006 a stela (fig. 5) came

FIGURE 5 The stela of the high priest of Amun, Bakenkhonsu B, dated to Year 4 of Sethnakhte; from Avenue of Sphinxes, Luxor.

to light that raised Sethnakhte's hitherto highest date from Year 2, III *šmw* 24[9] to some time in Year 4.[10] This stela had been erected by Bakenkhonsu (B), high priest of Amun at Karnak (see, further, page 52, below), and commemorates the re-erection of statues that had been displaced in some kind of disturbance—most probably the recent civil wars. On the assumption that Year 4 was Sethnakhte's last,[11] his death would have occurred on its I *šmw* 26, which is known to have been the accession day of his son and successor Rameses III.[12]

A smooth transition on the civil side to Sethnakhte's regime will doubtless have been aided by the continuation in office of the long-serving vizier Hori I, while in Nubia the viceroy Hori II also continued in post, erecting a stela at Amara West.[13] out in the Sinai a stela was inscribed in honor of the king by the officials Amenopet and Sethy S in the temple of Hathor at Serabit el-Khadim.[14] Other surviving monuments of Sethnakhte's reign include the addition of the king's cartouches to monuments at Nabesha, Heliopolis, Memphis, and Karnak.[15] In addition, chapel E at the so-called Oratory of Ptah near Deir el-Medina was usurped from Amenmeses and Sethy II, with chapel D perhaps begun by Sethnakhte: it ultimately became a joint memorial of Sethnakhte and Rameses III (fig. 31).[16]

On his accession, Rameses III, like any Egyptian king, was faced with the need to bury his father. In this he had a problem in that the tomb begun for Sethnakhte in the Valley of the Kings, KV11 (figs. 6, 7, 94),[17] was unfinished. It had been begun in the central area of the Valley, to the right of the sepulcher of the defeated usurper Amenmeses (KV10), and after progressing for some thirty meters had run into the ceiling of the latter (figs. 8, 9). Clearly, this will have caused delay while some replanning was undertaken, the axis being shifted to the right and given a slight upward slope to ensure that the new floor was well clear of the adjacent tomb (figs. 7, 94, vestibule D1, corridor D2).

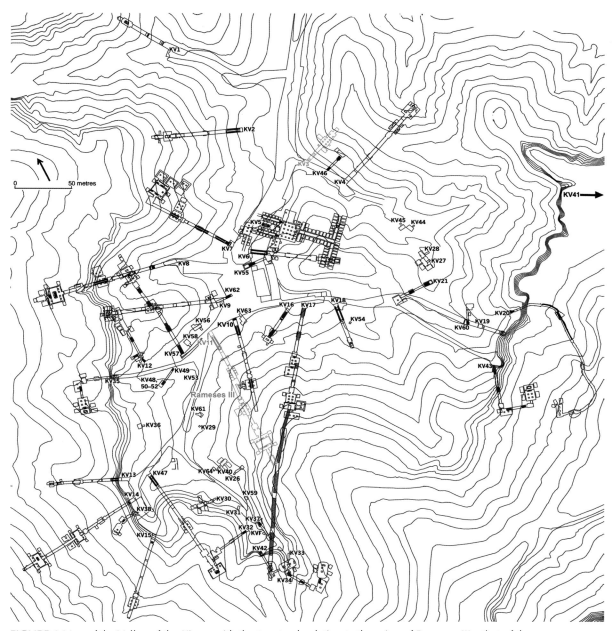

FIGURE 6 Map of the Valley of the Kings, with the two tombs dating to the reign of Rameses III—that of the king himself (KV11, begun by Sethnakhte) and that of an anonymous prince (KV3)—highlighted in red.

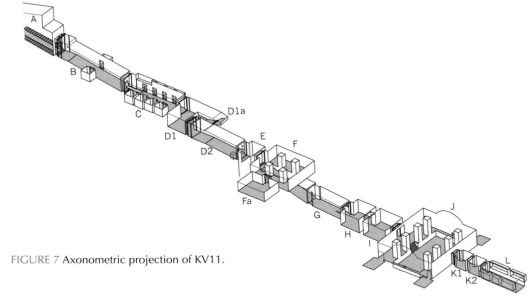

FIGURE 7 Axonometric projection of KV11.

FIGURE 8 Corridors B and C of KV11,
decorated under Sethnakhte with
the Litany of Re and Book of *Amduat*.

FIGURE 9 The unfinished corridor D1a: this is the point
at which the quarrymen broke through into an unfinished
side chamber of the adjacent KV10 (Amenmeses).

FIGURE 10 The left pair of the unique bovid-headed pilasters at the entrance to KV11.

Although a pair of unique bovid-headed pilasters flanked the very entrance (fig. 10), decoration otherwise had been begun in a conventional manner, with the customary solar disk and kneeling goddesses on the lintel, and scenes showing the king's welcome into the netherworld by Re-Horakhty at the beginning of corridor B. The rest of this corridor and the following corridor C were adorned with the Litany of Re and subsidiary figures, which had become standard in the royal tombs whose construction had immediately preceded that of KV11. The non-standard room D1 was adorned with figures of the king and the gods (fig. 11), before D2 again picked up the traditional *Amduat*-based scheme. However, only the jambs of the gate between D1 and D2 had been carved by the time that Sethnakhte died, although D2 had probably been quarried in its entirety when the king's death brought work to a halt.

FIGURE 11 Chamber D1 in KV11, created to allow the tomb's axis to be shifted to the right following the accidental penetration into KV10. Decorated for Sethnakhte, all cartouches were later altered to those of Rameses III.

FIGURE 12 In the outer part of KV14, images of Tawosret were covered in plaster and recarved as Sethnakhte. This plaster has fallen away, revealing the way in which the images began as Tawosret as queen, were then altered to show her as female king, and finally changed to depict Sethnakhte. In addition, the depictions of Siptah and Sethy II in the tomb all had their cartouches altered to those of Sethnakhte.

Although chamber D1 was large enough to have accommodated a burial, Rameses III actually buried his father in Tawosret's presumably unoccupied KV14. Clearly, all modifications were carried out during the restricted period allowed by Sethnakhte's mummification, as attempts to rework images of Tawosret were essentially limited to only the first corridor of the tomb (fig. 12). In contrast, her remaining figures were simply covered with plaster and just Sethnakhte's names and titles drawn in black on the unpainted plaster—or, very occasionally, the king's actual figure sketched in outline

FIGURE 13 Deeper inside KV14, Tawosret's figures were again covered with plaster, but in most cases no attempt was made to carve new images. Rather, ink was used to simply add Sethnakhte's names and titles (bottom), or in a few cases to draw a figure of the tomb's new owner (top: as shown on the pillar in chamber K, Tawosret's intended burial chamber as queen).

FIGURE 14 The heavily restored main burial chamber of KV14, created by Tawosret during her final two years of power, as female pharaoh. The decoration was never finished, and the sarcophagus (made for King Tawosret and the cartouches reinscribed for Sethnakhte) was smashed in antiquity.

(fig. 13); the name of a queen Sitre-[ta]meri (presumably a wife of Sethnakhte) was also substituted for that of Tawosret in one place. In addition, the images of Siptah and Sethy II in the tomb had their cartouches altered to those of Sethnakhte, as were those on Tawosret's sarcophagus (fig. 14). It seems likely that Sethnakhte had himself appropriated the memorial temple of Tawosret, as it appears to have been fully completed, in spite of its foundation deposits being dated to the last year of the latter's reign.[18]

2 THE REIGN AND MONUMENTS OF RAMESES III

Becoming Pharaoh

As king, Rameses III took the usual five-fold titulary, the 'core' form of which was:

Horus
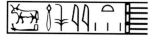

kȝ-nḫt ʿȝ-nsyt
Strong bull, great in kingship

Nebti

wr-ḥbw-sd mi tȝ-ṯnn
Great of jubilees like Tatjenen

Golden Falcon

wsr-rnpwt mi itmw
Rich in years like Atum

Prenomen

wsr-mȝʿt-rʿ mry-imn
The strong one of the Maat of Re, beloved of Amun

Nomen

rʿ-mss ḥqȝ-iwnw
The one born of Re, the ruler of Heliopolis

However, like most kings since the middle of the Eighteenth Dynasty, Rameses employed a range of alternate or extended Horus, Nebti, and Golden Falcon names, in particular in and around his complex at Medinet Habu (for which see pages 83–99, below), where fourteen additional Horus names are to be found.[1]

In his choice of names, the third Rameses clearly looked back to Rameses II as a model. Previously, it had been unusual for a king to reuse the prenomen of a predecessor, although ones closely modeled on preceding examples were not uncommon (for example, Akheper*ka*re, Akheper*en*re, and Akheper*u*re, used respectively by Thutmose I, Thutmose II, and Amenhotep II). However, Rameses III took the basic prenomen of Rameses II, Usermaatre, without change, although swapping the earlier king's epithet, "setepenre," for "meryamun." His Horus, Nebti, and Golden Falcon names had all also been used by the earlier king, as had the epithet in the nomen, although in Rameses II's case the latter had been only an occasional addition, and always alongside his core nomen of Rameses-meryamun.

These choices had clear political import, especially in light of the events of the previous two decades, and Rameses III's close imitation of Rameses II must have been with the firm intent of linking himself with the last era of peace and stability. Sethnakhte had clearly had a similar motive in employing the same Horus name as Sethy II, and a prenomen based on that of the same pharaoh, the last indisputably 'legitimate' ruler of the Nineteenth Dynasty line. That Sethy II was regarded as the 'official' predecessor of the new dynasty is clear in depictions carved under Rameses III, which show statues of his predecessors carried in the procession of the Festival of Min: these jump directly from Sethy II to Sethnakhte.

This implicit attempt to link himself with Rameses II is also to be seen in the names that Rameses III assigned to his sons in some cases, and even then inconsistently, prefixed with the name 'Rameses,' which mirrored those of senior sons of the earlier pharaoh, with even titles assigned on the basis of those held by the previous princes so named. For example, Rameses III's son Khaemwaset (E) was made *Sem*-priest of Ptah, the office long held by perhaps the best-known of all Rameses II's sons, Khaemwaset C, whose fame lasted until Ptolemaic times.[2]

Rameses the Builder

Although by no means as prolific a builder as his namesake and inspiration, Rameses III undertook a considerable amount of building and restoration, a range of sites being mentioned in a retrospective of his gifts to the gods in pHarris I (see, further, page 80–81, below), with significant structures surviving at Thebes, and lesser remains throughout Egypt.

Starting in the north, the papyrus records work at the temple of Seth at Per-Rameses, a site at which little survives other than foundation trenches, although a stela of the king was found there; Tanis, to which many architectural elements and statuary were moved from Per-Rameses during the Third Intermediate Period, has also yielded statues of Rameses

III. Perhaps also originally from Per-Rameses are a doorjamb from Tell Moqdam and a statue base from Bubastis,[3] while pHarris I records a restoration of the temple of Horus-Khentykhet at Athribis.

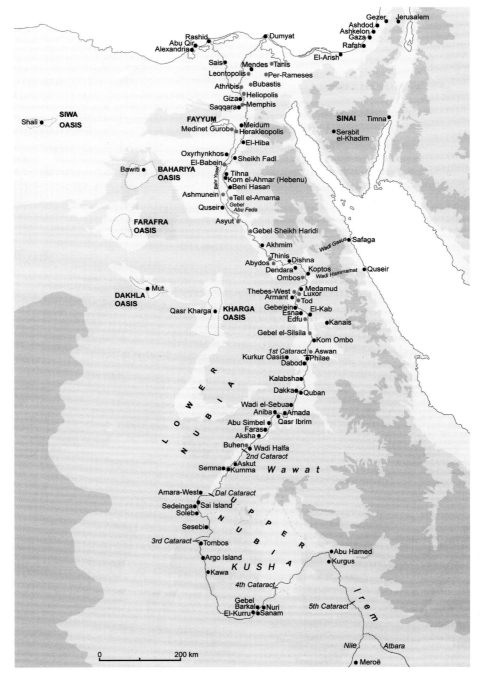

FIGURE 15 Map of Egypt and Nubia, with the principal sites with material of Rameses III marked in red.

Extensive work is recorded in the temples at Heliopolis, including colossal statuary, now represented by various fragments of architecture and statuary.[4] Likewise, major benefactions are claimed at Memphis, including a new (or rebuilt) temple, and a range of other restorations and rebuilding, but only a few columns and an added inscription have thus far come to light.[5] To the west of Memphis, a burial of the sacred Apis bull has been attributed to the reign of Rameses III, but the evidence for the dating is unclear.[6] In the Fayyum area, an endowment stela from the area of Herakleopolis and inlays from Medinet Gurob bear the names of the third Rameses.[7]

A number of rock stelae of the king are to be found in Middle Egypt, with examples at the chapel of Merenptah at el-Babein, at Tihna, and at Khazindariya (Gebel Sheikh Haridi), all associated with limestone quarries (fig. 16).[8] Activity at the site of Tell el-Amarna is indicated by the presence of Rameses III's name on a block from the so-called River Temple there, which would appear to have been a Ramesside foundation, on the site of a structure of the Amarna Period.[9] Also in the region, pHarris I describes benefactions and building work at Ashmunein and Asyut, but only a stela from the former site is known.[10] Of work described at Thinis, Abydos, and Ombos, all that survives are additions of the king's name to gateways in the temples of Sethy I and Rameses II at the latter site.[11]

Thebes (fig. 72) hosts not only Rameses III's greatest monument, his West Theban memorial complex at Medinet Habu, which will be dealt with in detail in chapter 4, and his tomb (and those of his family: see pages 60–68), but also buildings, sculpture (fig. 17), and added inscriptions at Karnak, together with minor works at Luxor temple, the Ramesseum, and Deir el-Medina. Five Theban temples are actually mentioned in pHarris I: the Medinet Habu complex; the House-of-Rameses-heqaon-in-the-House-of-Amun (the 'bark temple' in the First Courtyard at Karnak: see just below); the House-of-Rameses-heqaon-in-the-House-of-Khonsu (see pages 23–25, below); the Temple-of-Rameses-heqaon-Possessed-of-Joy-in-Karnak (possibly the South Temple in the Precinct of Mut: see pages 25–26, below); and the House-of-Usermaatre-meryamun-in-the-House-of-Amun (likewise).

At the time Rameses came to the throne, the temple of Amun at Karnak terminated at Pylon II, with the Nile bank not far west of the line now marked by Pylon I (fig. 19).[12] In this open space, close to what would have been the quayside, Sethy II had built a triple shrine at right angles to, and north of, the main axis of the temple, to accommodate the barks of Amun, Mut, and Khonsu when they 'rested' while leaving or re-entering the Karnak precinct during such events as the Beautiful Feast of the Valley (see page 78). Now, closer to the façade of the main temple, and to the south of the principal axis, Rameses III built his House-of-Rameses-heqaon-in-the-House-of-Amun as a much

FIGURE 16 Provincial memorials of Rameses III in Middle Egypt; top: Tihna; bottom: Gebel Sheikh Haridi.

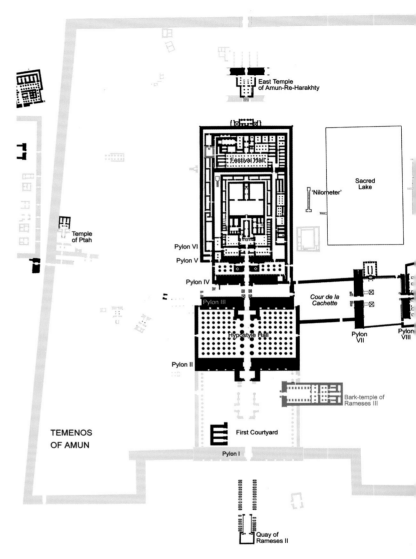

FIGURE 18 Plan of Karnak, with the principal works of Rameses III shown in red.

FIGURE 17 A colossal statue of Rameses III; from the Karnak cachette (Cairo JE41749=CG42149).

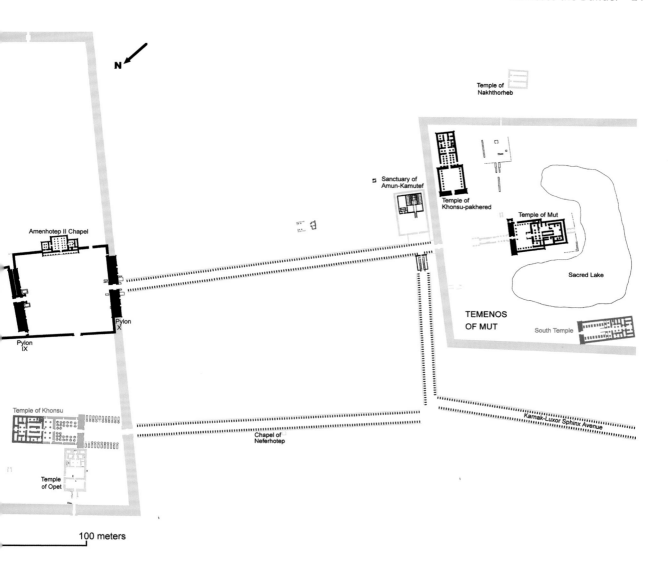

N

Temple of
Nakhthorheb

Sanctuary of
Amun-Kamutef

Temple of
Khonsu-pakhered

Temple of Mut

Amenhotep II Chapel

Sacred Lake

Pylon
X

TEMENOS
OF MUT

South Temple

Pylon
IX

Temple of Khonsu

Karnak-Luxor Sphinx Avenue

Chapel of
Neferhotep

Temple
of Opet

100 meters

larger resting place for the divine barks, in the form of a fully-fledged small temple.[13] It would appear to have been built during the second half of the king's reign, but the standard of workmanship is generally inferior to that seen at Medinet Habu.

In plan, the structure follows the standard basic plan of a Ramesside temple, with a pylon fronting a peristyle court, with each pier fronted by a standing figure of the king (fig. 20). Beyond is a four-columned portico and hypostyle hall, with the chapels for the barks of the three deities to the rear. Apart from the stereotyped smiting scenes on the pylon, the decoration of the bark temple reflects its role as a venue for components of festivals, with the eastern half of the peristyle court adorned with scenes of the Festival

FIGURE 19 The First Court at Karnak, showing the bark temple of Rameses III, flanked by the Bubastite Portal and colonnade, both constructed by Shoshenq I.

FIGURE 20 The west side of the peristyle court of Rameses III's bark temple.

FIGURE 21 Rameses III offering to the bark of Amun, in the central shrine of his bark temple.

of Amun, and the western half of the Festival of Min. The hypostyle has the king offering
to various deities, while the chapels focus on the king before the respective barks (fig.
21). The exterior of the building is mainly concerned with offerings to the gods, with the
exception of one tableau, at the northern end of the western wall, which concerns the
king's victory over Syrian and Libyan enemies (cf. pages 35–37, 43–45, below).

One hundred twenty meters to the south of the bark temple is the House-of-
Rameses-heqaon-in-the-House-of-Khonsu (fig. 22).[14] Although laid out under Rameses
III, only three subsidiary rooms of the innermost part seem to have been decorated
during his lifetime (fig. 23). The rest of the rear section was adorned under Rameses
IV, with the hypostyle hall not decorated until late in the reign of Rameses XI, and
the peristyle court and pylon not until the beginning of the Twenty-first Dynasty,
by Herihor and Panedjem I, respectively. The exterior of the temple did not receive
decoration until the Thirtieth and Ptolemaic dynasties. The temple made extensive use
of blocks taken from other monuments, at least some coming from the memorial temple

FIGURE 22 The temple of Khonsu at Karnak, begun by Rameses III and continued by his successors, with the decoration not completed until the early Twenty-first Dynasty.

FIGURE 23 Rameses III offering flowers to Montju in Room XII of the Khonsu temple; Hathor is shown behind him.

of Horemheb (some already reused from that of Tutankhamun) on the West Bank—directly next to Rameses III's own memorial complex, which may have facilitated the robbing of stone from the more ancient structure.[15] Material also came from buildings of Sethy I, Merenptah, and Sethy II.[16]

Rameses III founded another temple some five hundred meters south of the Khonsu temple, within the Precinct of Mut, wife of Amun and mother of Khonsu (fig. 24). The suggestion that this may have been pHarris I's Temple-of-Rameses-heqaon-Possessed-of-Joy-in-Karnak has been based on it being the southernmost of Rameses's Karnak temples, and further characterized in the papyrus as being in "Southern Opet."[17] However, the latter is normally a term for the area of Luxor temple, two kilometers further south, and the Temple-of-Rameses-heqaon-Possessed-of-Joy-in-Karnak may thus have been a now-vanished structure associated with the Luxor temple (where Rameses III certainly did work: see below), leaving what is now referred to as the South Temple as most probably the House-of-Usermaatre-meryamun-in-the-House-of-Amun. In the Precinct of Mut and in the South Temple itself[18] the goddess was simply Amun's consort.

The temple is in poor condition; only a few courses of its walls survive, although enough to show that it conformed to a similar plan to the bark temple, albeit with a

FIGURE 24 The South Temple in the Precinct of Mut at Karnak.

somewhat different arrangement of its inner rooms. Its state makes it difficult to say much about the temple's decoration, apart from the presence of fragments of scenes of the king and the gods, plus blocks from a Libyan triumph scene in the northwest corner of the peristyle court, and Libyan and Syrian war scenes on the west exterior wall.

Besides his five new Theban temples, Rameses III added a number of minor elements to the main Amun-temple. In particular, he added a now largely destroyed structure to the northern end of the courtyard between Pylons III and IV (fig. 25), redecorated the high-level solar shrine (Room XXXV) on the north side of the Festival Hall (usurping Amenmeses) and much of the court between Pylons VII and VIII, including the back of Pylon VIII and the colossi in front of Pylon VII (figs. 26, 27, 28), and added cartouches and a tableau between Pylons V and VI (fig. 29), as well as to the back of Pylon IX.

In addition, the king added texts and/or his cartouches in numerous other locations, including the columns of the central aisle of the Great Hypostyle Hall, the rear of Pylon III, in the doorway of Pylon IV, at the base of the girdle wall of the rear part of the temple, and the inner walls of the court between Pylons IX and X. A number of these

FIGURE 25 The area between Pylon III and Pylon IV at Karnak, the location of a now largely lost structure of Rameses III.

FIGURE 26 The north end of the inside of the east wall of the court between Pylons VII and VIII at Karnak, showing one of the added scenes of Rameses III. To its right is the bark shrine of Thutmose III.

FIGURE 27 Detail of the rear (north face) of Pylon VIII at Karnak, originally built under Hatshepsut and Thutmose III, which had various scenes added by later kings. These included a series showing Rameses III in the company of various deities; here he is shown with Thoth, offering Maat to Re-Horakhty and Iusas.

FIGURE 28 The western colossus on the south side of Pylon VII, with an added image and text of Rameses III.

added texts are alongside similar ones of Rameses IV, and these may be posthumous commemorations of Rameses III by his son. Base texts of Rameses III (on his own) are also to be found at Luxor temple, along with some other decorative additions, particularly on the exterior walls of the original inner temple of Amenhotep III (fig. 30).

FIGURE 29 Scene of Rameses III on the south wall of the antechamber of Pylon VI at Karnak.

FIGURE 30 The eastern exterior wall of the rear section of the Luxor temple was decorated by Rameses III, although this work was never completed. This part shows the king being led by Atum and another god on the left, and purified by Horus(?) and Thoth on the right.

FIGURE 31 The so-called Oratory of Ptah, on the path between the Valley of the Queens and Deir el-Medina, with various chapels and stelae marked.

On the West Bank, other than work on his own Medinet Habu foundation, Rameses III's cartouches were added to the bases of several colossi at the Ramesseum, while the Oratory of Ptah (fig. 31), where late–Nineteenth Dynasty kings and Sethnakhte had been active (cf. page 31, above), stelae of the king and a Prince Amenhirkopeshef were added to chapel G, while the viziers Hori and To (see page 50, below) dedicated chapels A, B, C, and D , including depictions of the king.[19]

South of Thebes, perhaps the most significant remains of Rameses III are the pylon of the temple of Horus at Edfu, within the later Ptolemaic temple (fig. 32).[20] Elsewhere, activity under Rameses III is indicated by the addition of names and texts to earlier monuments, such as the bark shrine at Tod,[21] and stelae and graffiti added in the rock temple at Gebel Silsila[22] and in the South Temple at Buhen, deep in Nubia.[23] Nothing is known from further south, but Egyptian activity at Kawa is attested under Rameses IV,[24] and at Amara West until the reign of Rameses IX.[25]

The Foreign Policy and Wars of Rameses III

Extensive lists of foreign polities survive from the monuments of Rameses III but, as is so often the case with such lists, their equation and location can be problematic. Likewise often unclear is their status (conquests, allies, places of strategic interest?) and currency (directly relevant to the author or stereotyped copying from earlier lists?).[26] Other overseas links, specifically to the Aegean, are suggested by the depiction of Late Helladic IIIC stirrup jars in the king's tomb (fig. 100b).

However, it is clear that the international situation was by no means as stable as had been the case two centuries earlier, where a "concert of great powers" had kept the Near East in relative equilibrium.[27] Then, expansion by the Hittites had led to the effective extinction of the northwest Syrian "great power," Mitanni, and then conflict with the Egyptians over relative spheres of suzerainty in northern Syria. This had culminated in the Battle of Qadesh, fought by Rameses II, and then a peace treaty agreed between the Egyptians and the Hittites in Rameses's Year 21.

This Egypto-Hittite entente may have been influenced by changes in surrounding territories, especially the resurgence of Assyria, whose Middle Empire was consolidating its authority east of the Euphrates. There also, seemingly, were changes underway in the northeastern part of the Mediterranean basin, evidenced by the involvement of groups apparently from here in an attempted invasion of Egypt from Libya in Year 5 of Merenptah. This incursion had reached "Perire," a place of imprecise location, but certainly in the southern part of the western Delta, before being stopped by the Egyptians. These events were recorded in the king's Great Karnak Inscription and associated reliefs in the Cour de la cachette in the temple of Amun-Re at Karnak.[28]

FIGURE 32 The remains of the pylon of the New Kingdom temple of Horus at Edfu, including texts of Rameses III (one dated to Year 15 and decreeing increased offerings for all temples in the south of Egypt) and Rameses IV. The temple was demolished when the forecourt of the present temple was built at right angles to, and across, its axis under Ptolemy IX and XII; the pylon in the background dates to the latter reign.

These apparently northeast Mediterranean elements are named by Merenptah as the "Eqwesh" (*iq3w3š3*), "Shekelesh" (*š3krš3*), Sherden [*š3rdn*], "Lukka" (*lkw*), and "Teresh" (*twrš3*), with the first three characterized as "of the countries of the sea," contributing to their all being dubbed 'Sea Peoples' in modern times. The Lukka are known from earlier texts, both Egyptian and Hittite, which imply that they came from southwest Anatolia, conforming to a general assumption that their homeland was none other than the Lycia that was located in this area in classical times.[29]

FIGURE 33 The Mediterranean.

Similar attempts have been made to link the other toponyms with later entities of the Mediterranean region,[30] the Teresh being linked with the later Tyrrhenians, who have been placed on the western side of the Italian peninsula. The origins of the Sherden, known from documentation going back to the late New Kingdom, where they appear as maritime mercenaries, have also been placed in this area, perhaps on the island of Sardinia. The "Shekelesh" have been proposed as Sicilians, and the "Eqwesh" as the Homeric Achaeans/Hittite Akhkhiyawa—most likely Mycenaean Greece. While none of these equations can yet be objectively proved, none seem intrinsically unlikely, and the existence of displaced elements from mainland Greece would tie in with widespread horizons of destruction and abandonment seen in the Mycenaean heartland during Late Helladic IIIC, the first half of the twelfth century. Given that the attack is described as only coming from the west, one must assume that the Sea Peoples element must have previously crossed to Libya to become part of the invading force. This would be in accordance with the prevailing currents and winds in the eastern Mediterranean, which could bring vessels from the western Aegean and the area of Crete across to Cyrenaica, and then along the Libyan coast toward Egypt.

Acts of war

In pHarris I, Rameses III's principal warlike activities are enumerated as follows:

> I extended all the boundaries of Egypt; I overthrew those who invaded them from their lands. I slew the Denyen [*dnnw*] in their isles, the Tjeker [*ṯkrw*] and the Peleset [*plstw*] were made ashes. The Sherden and the Weshesh [*wššw*] of the sea, they were made as those that do not exist, taken captive at one time, brought as captives to Egypt, like the sand of the shore. I settled them in strongholds, bound in my name. Numerous were their classes like hundred-thousands. I taxed them all, in clothing and grain from the storehouses and granaries each year.
>
> I destroyed the people of Saru [*s'rw*], of the tribes of the Shasu [*š3sw*]; I plundered their tents of their people, their possessions, their cattle likewise, without number. They were pinioned and brought as captive, as tribute of Egypt. I gave them to the gods, as slaves into their house[s].
>
> See, I will inform you of other things, done in Egypt since my reign. The Libu [*lbw*] and the Meshwesh [*mššw*] were dwelling in Egypt, having plundered the cities of the western border, from Memphis to *q3r3b3n3*. They had reached the great river on both its banks. It was them who plundered the cities of *gwtwty* during very many years, while they were in Egypt. Behold, I destroyed them, slain at one time. I laid low the Meshwesh, the Libu, the Isbet [*isbtw*], the Qeyqesh [*qyqšw*], the Shaytpu/Shydjdju [*šytpw/šyḏḏw*], the Hes [*hsw*] and the Beqen [*bqnw*]; they were overthrown in their blood and made heaps. I turned them back from trampling the border of Egypt. I carried away those whom my sword spared, as numerous captives, pinioned like birds before my horses, their wives and their children by the ten-thousand, their cattle in number like hundred-thousands. I settled their leaders in strongholds in my name. I gave to them captains of archers, and chief men of the tribes, branded and made into slaves, impressed with my name; their wives and their children were made likewise. I led their cattle into the house of Amun; they were made for him into herds forever.[31]

The military activities mentioned in this text are all illustrated in reliefs in Rameses III's temples, in particular at Medinet Habu.[32] The fact that other such activities, not mentioned in pHarris I, are also shown in reliefs has been used to query whether the latter actually happened, or were simply elaborate evocations of what a king *should* do.

However, there is no evidence that pHarris I was intended to be exhaustive in its 'historical' narrative; rather, it seems more likely to have provided 'edited highlights' of Rameses III's international career. In particular, two separate Libyan wars are depicted on the monuments, and, as specifically dated to Years 5 and 11, would appear both to be 'genuine'—although there has been an attempt to deny the existence of the first of these pages 149–51, below). However, this kind of blatant falsification of the record seems without precedent, and there appears no real reason for doubting the reality of the two Libyan wars.

The First Libyan War

After Merenptah's victory against his foes from the west, no evidence survives of further problems from there during the latter years of the Nineteenth Dynasty, but, given the internal problems of this period, the lack of relevant texts makes the issue moot. In any case, in Year 5 of Rameses III there came a new Libyan threat (fig. 34), the first of a series of conflicts recorded in a series of texts and reliefs (fig. 35) in the king's memorial temple at Medinet Habu.[33]

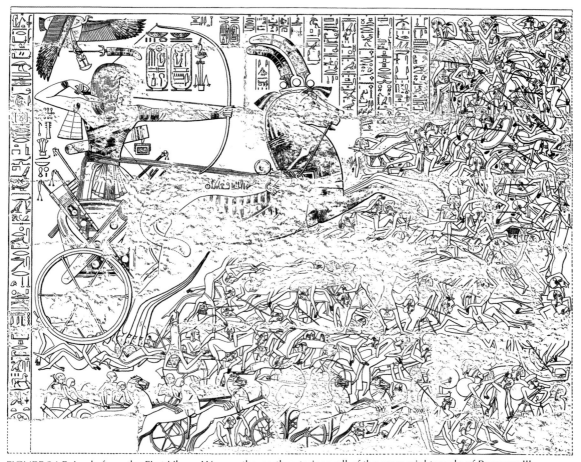

FIGURE 34 Episode from the First Libyan War, on the north exterior wall of the memorial temple of Rameses III.

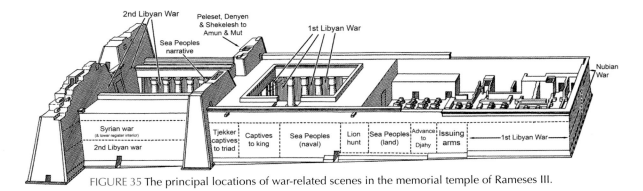

FIGURE 35 The principal locations of war-related scenes in the memorial temple of Rameses III.

The land of the Libyans [*tmḥw*] came, united in one place with even Libu, Seped [*spdw*], and Meshwesh levied from the lands of the Buriru [*bwrrw*](?). Their warriors relied upon their plan, coming with confident hearts: "We will advance ourselves!" Their counsels within their bodies were: "We will succeed!" Their hearts were full of malice, bringing subversion—but their plan was smashed and turned aside by the will of the god.[34]

It is presumably to the run-up to this first war that belongs the pHarris I narrative's detail that the enemy had previously been raiding settlements along the western margin of the Nile Delta. Q3r3b3n3 may have been near Abu Qir, perhaps to be equated with the "Karbaniti" in seventh-century Assyrian annals, and would certainly make an obvious northern terminus for a line running northwest from Memphis. This would be supported if *gwtwty*, noted as plundered by the Libyans, were to be Canopus (*pr-gw3ty*), close to Abu Qir.[35]

His Person thus went forth against them, like a flame through dense brushwood, and took them like birds in a net. They were threshed like sheaves, reduced to ashes, and cast down prostrate in their (own) blood. Their overthrow was heavy, and without limit: see, evil harried with them to the height of heaven. Their horde was gathered in at the place for their slaughter, they being made into pyramids on their (own) soil by the might of the King . . . . Every survivor was carried captive to Egypt, and hands and phalli beyond numbering presented as pinioned captives under the Window (of Royal Appearances).

The cutting of hands and genitalia from corpses was a standard means of keeping tally of those killed in battle, with clearly a humiliation aspect to the emasculation of corpses (fig. 36).

FIGURE 36 The counting and presentation to the king of severed hands to reckon the number of slain enemies after the First Libyan War, together with representative captives, as shown on the southeast wall of the Second Court.

The Sea Peoples

Three years later, in Year 8, came a further military challenge—but in this case from the east. The Medinet Habu texts set the scene thus:[36]

> The foreign countries made a conspiracy in their isles. Removed and scattered in battle were the lands at one time. No land could stand before their arms, beginning from Hatti: Qode, Carchemish, Arzawa and Alashia, cut off at [once] in one [place]. A camp was, pitched, in one place, within Amurru: they devastated its people and its land was like what had never existed. They came . . . on towards the Land of the Nile.
>
> Their alliance was: the Peleset, the Tjeker, the Shekelesh, the Den(u)<yen> and the Weshesh, lands united. They laid their hands on the lands to the circuit of the earth, their hearts trusting and confident: "Our plans succeed!"
>
> Now, the mind of (the king) . . . was prepared and ready to trap them like birds . . . . (He) organized (his) frontier in Djahy, prepared before them (local) chiefs, garrison-commanders, and *maryannu*-warriors. (He) caused the Nile mouth(s) to be prepared, as a strong rampart, with warships, (large) vessels and boats (all) prepared; they were manned completely, from stern to stern with valiant warriors bearing their weapons.
>
> The soldiery, of every picked man of the Land of the Nile, they were like lion(s) roaring upon the mountain-tops; the chariotry were (made up) of runners, of trained men(?), of every good and capable chariot-officer. Their horses were restless in every (part of) their bodies, ready to trample down the foreign countries under their hoofs.[37]

This account, combined with that in pHarris I (p. 14, above), provides the basis for all modern interpretations of the events of the year. As far as Rameses's antagonists listed in the two sources are concerned, three are familiar from the time of Merenptah, as are the Teresh, not mentioned at Medinet Habu or in pHarris I, but linked with the "new" Peleset in Rameses III's Stela C in the Oratory of Ptah at Deir el-Medina (for which see pages 30–31, above). Also new are the Denyen, Tjeker, and Weshesh.

Once again, no direct evidence exists to allow their places of origin to be determined, but the similarities in names have led to long-standing suggestions as to the identities in question.[38] Thus, the Denyen may be those referred to by Homer as the Danaeans, akin to the Achaeans, the Peleset may be the Biblical Philistines, the Tjeker were perhaps from the Levantine coast, near Haifa, or the Cretan town of Zakro, and the Weshesh were perhaps either the south Italian Osci or the south Palestinian Biblical tribe of Asher.

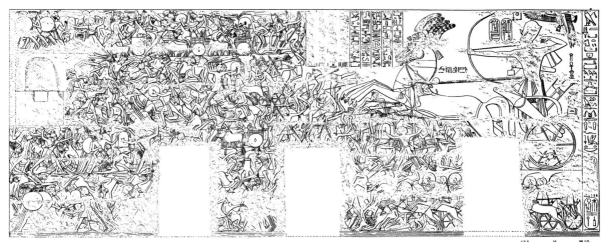

FIGURE 37 The land battle against the Sea Peoples (Medinet Habu, north wall).

However, it must be emphasized that no certainty attaches to any of these identifications, and thus that any interpretation based on them can only be regarded as a hypothesis.

Extensive reliefs on the northern exterior wall of Rameses III's memorial temple provide illustrations of the conflict. These begin with the issuing of arms to Egyptian troops by the king, and then the advance of the Egyptian forces into Djahy, the usual term for the region of Palestine between Ashkelon and Lebanon. Here, a battle is shown taking place against the enemy army (fig. 37), which is accompanied by oxcarts carrying women and children.[39]

An episode of lion-hunting by the king is then shown, perhaps to indicate his nonchalance at the forthcoming clash, or as a general indicator of his dominion over nature as well as human beings. This precedes an extensive tableau depicting a naval battle (fig. 38):

Now, indeed, the northern foreign countries that were in their islands were restless in their bodies; they penetrated the channels of the Nile mouths.

The scene is remarkable for its complexity and animation, with captives shown being led away along the shore, to end up in the final tableaux of the wall, with prisoners presented first to the king, and then with the Tjeker singled out for presentation to the Theban triad, together with a group of Libyan captives—presumably from the Year 5 campaign as they are not otherwise mentioned in the 'Sea Peoples' sequence. Also separated out are the Peleset, Denyen, and Shekelesh, presented to Amun and Mut on the south tower of the Second Pylon of the Medinet Habu temple, in parallel with the main narrative of the Sea Peoples campaign on the north tower (fig. 87).

FIGURE 38 The
sea battle against
the Sea Peoples
(Medinet Habu,
north wall).

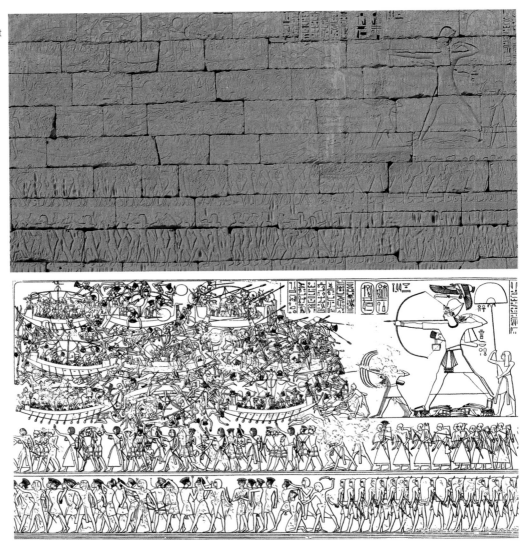

As for the fate of the captives, Rameses states in the pHarris I account that he "settled them in strongholds, bound in my name . . . . I taxed them all, in clothing and grain from the storehouses and granaries each year." Exactly where these "strongholds" were is not made clear, but many seem likely to have been along the Levantine coast, although some might have been in Egypt itself;[40] the Levant-settled Peleset have certainly been generally assumed to be the ancestors of the Biblical Philistines, although it has also been argued that their settlement in the area came slightly later.[41] That some were taken into Egyptian service is suggested by the appearance of figures who appear to be Peleset or Tjeker soldiers taking part in fighting in Nubia during Rameses III's reign.

The apocalyptic nature of the Sea Peoples' exploits as claimed in Rameses's text quoted at the beginning of this section have been linked with the numerous destructions to be found around the Levant at the beginning of the twelfth century. Ugarit was destroyed at some point soon after 1192 (date determined by the surviving record of an eclipse in that year),[42] and a letter found on the site has been used as evidence for the arrival of a hostile seaborne force directly before the destruction, on the basis of its having allegedly been found in a kiln. However, later research has suggested that the latter was probably not actually the case.[43] On the other hand, the text, addressed to the king of Cyprus, *does* state that "the ships of the enemy have come . . . setting fire to cities and have done harm to the land," so that the idea that seaborne enemies played a part in the end of Bronze Age Ugarit still seems valid. Various other sites in the area also have destruction levels, the one at Tell Tweini, a little way to the south, having produced a radiocarbon date of ca. 1080±14 BC.[44]

Inland in the same region, the site of Emar shows signs of destruction around the same time, with tablets mentioning "hordes," albeit without context.[45] Likewise, further south, a range of sites shows destruction layers from the early twelfth century, two (Deir Alla and Akko) with material naming Tawosret found in their destruction levels.[46] On the other hand, the sites of Lachish and Megiddo, although destroyed during the twelfth century, seem to have fallen around 1130, to judge from Egyptian Ramesside (including Rameses III) remains on site apparently predating the destruction.[47]

Moving northward into Anatolia, the Hittite capital at Boghazkale (Hattusa) shows clear signs of having been destroyed and abandoned early in the twelfth century, although the destruction of the public buildings may have followed their orderly vacation somewhat earlier. Anatolian destructions generally appear to be restricted to the northeastern part of the region,[48] and thus seem unlikely to have been victims of sea- or coast-based foes. The principal exception seems to be Troy, on the western coast of Anatolia, where the destruction of Troy VIIa has now been dated to around 1190–1180 BC.[49]

In the Aegean, almost all the Greek mainland polities, including Mycenae (fig. 39), Thebes, and Pylos, suffered destructions, while others were seemingly abandoned, during the late thirteenth and early twelfth centuries.[50] At Pylos, tablets dating to the moment of the palace's destruction by fire mention some kind of coast watch in operation. On Cyprus, however, destructions seem to be somewhat earlier than on the mainland, beginning around 1225, and may be unrelated to the mainland ones.[51] On the other hand, Alashia (Cyprus) is explicitly cited by Rameses III as having been one of the places impacted by the activity of the Sea Peoples.

This nexus of destructions throughout an arc from the Aegean through the Levant, during a period shortly before the Sea Peoples campaign of Rameses III, the latter described

FIGURE 39 Mycenae, the center of a major polity of the Greek Late Bronze Age, preserving evidence of interactions with Egypt going back to the late Eighteenth Dynasty. Like many such Aegean sites, Mycenae was burned during the early twelfth century BC.

by the pharaoh as coming at the end of the "remov[al] and scatter[ing] in battle [of] the lands at one time," has long suggested that they form parts of a connected whole. However, the lack of any concrete evidence for the identity of those responsible for any of these acts of destruction has led some more recent scholars to take a more skeptical approach and query whether they were only a factor in a wider range of natural and manmade causes.[52]

Probably the best solution is to see the battles between Rameses III and the Sea Peoples as the culmination of events that had unfolded over the previous few decades, comprising a mixture of natural events, local revolts, and local wars that produced displaced persons who sought new homes elsewhere and/or lent their maritime and military skills to other groups seeking conquest. Thus, an initial wave, produced by natural disasters in the Aegean and further west, lent their aid to the Libyans during their attack on Egypt during the reign of Merenptah, while further movements, produced by both the original natural disasters and the impact of the persons displaced by them (perhaps even to be classified as a systems collapse), led to a movement of peoples around the eastern end of the Mediterranean and through the Levant that ultimately threatened Egypt. If one follows the sequence of reliefs at Medinet Habu, an initial thrust against the land element was followed, after a gap, by a defensive battle somewhere around the Tanitic and Pelusiac mouths of the Nile.

The Second Libyan War

A text, found both on the rear of the First Pylon at Medinet Habu and on the interior of the west wall of Rameses III's Mut-precinct temple, and dated Year 11, IV *šmw* 10+x, describes in highly rhetorical terms another war against the Meshwesh, Tehenu, Libu, and Seped. Almost no detail, apart from the name of the Meshwesh chief, Kupuro, is provided amid the flowery prose praising Rameses III.[53] The text is supplemented by a number of texts and associated tableaux situated elsewhere on the rear of the First Pylon,[54] on the south inner wall of the First Court at Medinet Habu and west interior wall of the forecourt of the Mut-precinct temple,[55] on the exterior of the north wall between the First and Second Pylons at Medinet Habu (fig. 40),[56] on the exterior of the west wall of the king's bark temple at Karnak,[57] and on a stela in front of the Medinet Habu temple.[58]

FIGURE 40 Episode from the Second Libyan War (Medinet Habu, rear of the First Pylon).

It is presumably the aftermath of this second clash with the Libyans that is referred to in pHarris I's description of Rameses III settling them (like the Sea Peoples) "in strongholds in [his] name," giving them as slaves to his officers, and donating their cattle to the estate of Amun. Thus remaining in Egypt, it seems likely that these captives were ancestors of at least some of those of Libyan descent who were to play such an important role in the history of Egypt from the eleventh century onward.[59]

The Syrian War(s)

Undated are a series of further war reliefs, on the outer and inner faces of the north wall at Medinet Habu, between the pylons (the former above the Second Libyan War depictions), and another series on the exterior of the northern end of the west wall of the Karnak bark temple.[60] Nothing in their texts, banal in the extreme, indicates any reason for the conflict, but one may assume that they are related to pHarris I's narrative concerning the Shasu, which appears to be a generic term for various hostile groups in Palestine.

However, among Rameses's opponents are the inhabitants of "Tunip of Hatti" (fig. 41), Ullarza, and Amurru, with individuals of Hittite appearance shown defending a city in another scene. These are supplemented by the aforementioned (page 31) lists of toponyms, the most extensive of which accompany triumph scenes on the façade of the First Pylon at Medinet Habu (fig. 79);[61] five shorter ones also survive.[62] These lists include a considerable number of toponyms that may be identified as lying in the northern part of the Levant.[63]

A number of writers have dismissed these lists as mere copies of earlier works and, indeed, some have gone so far as to claim that that the 'Syrian War' was actually merely a minor action against 'nomads' in southern Palestine, or even wholly fictional (cf. pages 149–51, below). This latter view has been bolstered by the argument that the representations of 'Hittites' in the reliefs *must* be fictional, as the Hittite empire

FIGURE 41 The attack on Tunip during the Syrian War (Medinet Habu, north wall, between pylons).

had by then fallen. However, even after the dissolution of the empire, the acculturation of northern Syria would have been such that Hittite elements would remain there for a long time, with Neo-Hittite rump kingdoms arising there and enduring, in some cases, for centuries.[64] Indeed, Tunip seems essentially to be so described.

In addition, many of the toponyms in Rameses III's lists, especially that on the south tower of the First Pylon at Medinet Habu, are actually unique to Rameses III, and not found in any of the alleged earlier 'sources.' Even an apparent direct copy from Rameses II, the so-called Blessing of Ptah, on the front of the south tower of Medinet Habu's First Pylon,[65] includes a number of variations that show that the composition had been amended where necessary to accommodate current circumstance. Indeed, it is possible that both the Rameses II and Rameses III texts actually derive from a common earlier 'standard' source, rather than any direct copying of the text of Rameses II by the later king.

It should also be noted that various items bearing the name of Rameses III have been found in such Syro-Palestinian locations as Byblos and Megiddo, with a life-size statue (fig. 42) and an inscribed doorway in the king's name discovered at Beth Shan.[66] All this suggests a continued significant Egyptian presence in the middle part of the region throughout the reign of Rameses III, making operations significantly further north quite credible.

Accordingly, it seems that, presumably after defeating the Sea Peoples, and probably the Libyans for the second time (given the location of the Syrian reliefs below the Libyan ones: registers seem generally to be 'read' from bottom to top),[67] Rameses III undertook one or more campaigns that reached into northern Syria. Such an act would make sense to try to enhance Egypt's security by creating a buffer zone between 'near-abroad' Palestine and the presumably still-disordered lands in the further north and northwest, where a 'dark age' was descending and would remain in place in parts of the Aegean until the ninth century.[68]

FIGURE 42 Statue of Rameses III, from Beth Shan (Rockefeller S886).

Year 12 may have marked the end of Rameses III's active military operations. The earlier campaigns were celebrated explicitly or implicitly in two texts of that year, the aforementioned Blessing of Ptah and a pair of rhetorical stelae on the façade of the First Pylon at Medinet Habu.[69]

The Nubian War

An undated depiction of a Nubian conflict on the rear (west) wall of the Medinet Habu memorial temple[70] (fig. 43) has also been viewed with skepticism, especially as no such activity is mentioned in pHarris I. The tableaux in question are wholly generic, and lack any 'factual' data that might confirm their basis in reality, except that mercenaries, who by their appearance seem to be Peleset or Tjeker, are included, something not found in the earlier examples of such scenes.[71] Given that many Egyptian kings had to carry out police actions in Nubia, it would seem not unlikely that Rameses III had to undertake some kind of military activity there. These tableaux are thus most probably built on some reality, whether or not they represent a specific 'campaign' or an agglomeration of a number of ad hoc actions. Given that the Nubian tableaux would seem to have been carved at the same time as those relating to the First Libyan and Sea Peoples campaigns, the campaign may also have taken place during the first decade or so of the reign, after Year 8, if the presence of Peleset/Tjeker is to be taken seriously.

Acts of peace

Following on from its account of Rameses III's wars, pHarris I continues with further overseas activities:

> I made a very great well in the country of Ayna. It was surrounded by a wall like a mountain of gritstone, with 20 courses in the ground foundation, and a height of 30 cubits, having battlements. Its door posts and doors were hewn of cedar, their bolts were of copper, with mountings.
>
> I hewed great galleys with barges before them, manned with numerous crews, and attendants in great number; their captains of marines were with them, with inspectors and petty officers, to command them. They were laden with the products of Egypt without number, being in every number in ten-thousands. They were sent forth into the great sea of the Euphrates (Red Sea), they arrived at the countries of Punt, no mishap having overtaken them, safe and bearing awesomeness. The galleys and the barges were laden with the products of God's-Land, consisting of all the strange marvels of their country: plentiful myrrh of Punt, laden by ten-thousands, without number. Their chief's children of God's-Land went before their tribute, advancing

FIGURE 43 Depiction of the king attacking Nubians (Medinet Habu, rear wall).

to Egypt. They arrived in safety at the desert of Koptos (Wadi Hammamat); they landed in safety, bearing the things which they brought. They were loaded, on the land-journey, upon asses and upon men; and loaded into vessels upon the Nile, (at) the harbor of Koptos. They were sent forward downstream and arrived amid festivity, and brought (some) of the tribute into the (royal) presence like marvels. Their chief's children were in adoration before me, kissing the earth, prostrate before me. I gave them to all the gods of this land, to satisfy the two goddesses every morning.

I sent forth my messengers to the country of the Atika, to the great copper mines which are in this place. Their galleys carried them; others on the land-journey were upon their donkeys. It has not been heard before, since (before) kings reign(ed). Their mines were found abounding in copper; it was loaded by ten-thousands into their galleys. They were sent forward to Egypt and arrived safely. It was carried and made into a heap under the balcony, in many bars of copper, in hundred-thousands, being of the three times the color of gold. I allowed all the people to see them, like wonders.

I sent forth butlers and officials to the malachite-country, to my mother, Hathor, mistress of the malachite. There were brought for her silver, gold, royal linen, *mk*-linen, and many things into her presence, like the sand. There were brought for me wonders of real malachite in numerous sacks, brought forward into my presence. They had not been seen before, since (before) kings reign(ed).[72]

The location of Ayna and its well remains unknown, although the fact that one can locate the places subsequently mentioned to the east would suggest somewhere in the Eastern Desert, perhaps to support expeditions in that direction. Punt, whose location on the coast of the Red Sea remains a matter for debate, had been a destination for Egyptian trading expeditions since at least the time of Sahure in the Fifth Dynasty. Most views propose placing it somewhere along the coast, from the area of Port Sudan down to the Horn of Africa, although the southwest of the Arabian Peninsula has also been suggested.[73] The pHarris I text confirms that, at least during Rameses III's time, Koptos was the point at which such expeditions regained the Nile Valley, indicating that the Eastern Desert was traversed via the Wadi Hammamat, with Quseir as the Red Sea port employed.[74]

From the mention of its copper mines, Atika is almost certainly to be identified with Timna,[75] just north of the Gulf of Aqaba at the top of the Red Sea. Activity there by Rameses III is attested by a rock stela, recording the arrival of the butler Ramesesemperre, and faience fragments,[76] while a monumental pair of cartouches at Nahal Roded, just to the southwest, may be a way-marker connected with it. There is also material on the ground at the turquoise/malachite mines at Serabit el-Khadim, in the form of a stela of Year 23 (fig. 44),[77] to verify Rameses III's activity there. Connections even further east are indicated by further monumental cartouches at Tayma in the heart of Arabia.[78]

Because his reign exceeded three decades, one would have expected Rameses III to have celebrated a *ḥb-sd* jubilee, generally (but by no means exclusively) celebrated after thirty years on the throne.[79] However, no official monument contains any record of such an occasion, although its celebration is confirmed by two complementary sources. In one, we read that on IV *prt* 28 of Year 29, "the vizier To sailed northwards, after he had come to take the gods of Upper Egypt to the *ḥb-sd*."[80] This ties in with a fragmentary scene in the tomb-chapel of Setau, high priest of Nekhbet at el-Kab (EK4), which shows a procession of boats, with the label text dated to Year 29 of Rameses III and captioned as relating to the "first occasion of the *ḥb-sd*," with the vizier To commanded to bring the bark of Nekhbet northward from el-Kab to Per-Rameses to take part in the celebration there (fig. 45).[81] The lack of monumental attestation of the festival may reflect the problematic state of the country at the time: To's activities coincide closely with the strikes and protests that broke out in Western Thebes that year (see pages 54–55, below).

FIGURE 44 Serabit el-Khadim, with a stela from the site dated to Year 23, and showing Rameses III offering to Hathor.

FIGURE 45 The bark of the goddess Nekhbet proceeding northward to participate in the jubilee of Rameses III, as shown in the tomb-chapel of Setau at el-Kab (EK4).

The Officers of State

Two viziers are known to have served under Rameses III. The first, Hori I, the great-grandson of Rameses II (page 3, above), had been in office since the latter part of the reign of Sethy II, first alongside Preemheb and then apparently as sole vizier from early in the time of Siptah.[82] As such, he was the great survivor of the age, living through the era of Bay and Tawosret, and presumably had backed Sethnakhte in the final civil war. It is unclear how long Hori's career lasted under Rameses III, but before Year 16 he had been succeeded by To (at least in the south),[83] who, as we have already seen, was still in office in Year 29, when he was given the northern vizierate as well.[84] To is unattested under Rameses IV, in whose Year 2 one Neferrenpet is known to have been vizier.[85] pHarris I records the deposition of a rebellious vizier at Athribis,[86] but he seems unlikely to have been either Hori or To, given that their monuments remain undamaged.

In Nubia, two further Horis, father (II, fig. 46)[87] and son (III),[88] served as viceroy under Rameses III. Hori II, son of a certain Kama, had been appointed between Years 3 and 6 of Siptah, and served Rameses III until sometime before Year 5, when the younger Hori is known to have been in office. Hori III would go on to serve Rameses IV, and be buried at Bubastis (fig. 47). A number of subordinates of the viceroys are known, ranging from a mayor of Buhen, Hormose, and a troop commander, Bakenseth, through to scribes, messengers, and musicians.[89]

Hardly any other administrative officials are attested from the reign of Rameses III, reflecting in part the small number of tomb-chapels that survive at Thebes from the latter part of the New Kingdom: these are a major source of data on officialdom

FIGURE 46 Lintel from Buhen, showing a viceroy Hori (probably II) and the mayor of Buhen Hormose adoring the cartouches of Rameses III (BM EA66667 + Khartoum[?]).

FIGURE 47 The tomb of Hori III at Bubastis and his granite anthropoid coffin that was found in it (Cairo JE49612).

of earlier periods. Presumably most senior officials were now being buried in the north, where even the decidedly 'southern' viceroys Hori II and III were interred. In addition, some tomb-chapels were now freestanding structures, and thus more liable to destruction, for example that of the mayor of Thebes, Paser, whose chapel once lay at Medinet Habu, but is now represented only by blocks reused nearby.[90] On the other hand, a few officials belonging to the royal estates are known,[91] as are various army and logistics personnel,[92] while a significant number of holders of priestly office have left memorials.

At Karnak, the high priest Bakenkhonsu B, the son of the general Amenemopet, had, as already noted above (page 8), been in office since at least the reign of Sethnakhte.[93] He served until sometime before Year 26, when an Usermaatrenakhte is mentioned in an ostracon as holding the high priesthood.[94] It is uncertain how long the new man served, but by Year 1 of Rameses IV he had been succeeded by Ramesesnakhte, the son of Merybast, a Hermopolitan finance official. This new pontiff would remain in office until at least Year 2 of Rameses IX,[95] and would be followed in his role by two sons—and may have been an ancestor of the kings of the Twenty-first Dynasty.[96]

Of the lesser clergy of Amun, the office of Third Prophet was initially held by Tjanefer (TT158—fig. 48),[97] grandson-in-law of Bakenkhonsu, who was then followed in office before Year 27 (cf. page 69, below) by his son Amenemopet (TT148), who remained in the position until at least the reign of Rameses V.[98] The status of the family is illustrated by the scale of their tomb-chapels, that of Tjanefer incorporating a pyramid at the very peak of the southern end of the Dra Abu'l-Naga necropolis.

FIGURE 48 The southern peak of the Dra Abu'l-Naga hill, including the tomb-chapels of a number of the higher clergy of Amun during the Nineteenth and Twentieth Dynasties: that of the Third Prophet Tjanefer (TT158), with its pyramid on the summit, dates to the time of Rameses III. High priestly tombs include those of Bakenkhonsu A (TT35) and Nebwenenef (TT157, both under Rameses II), and Roma-Roy (TT283, Rameses II to Sethy II). Also in this location are the tombs of Paser (TT303, Third Prophet, late Twentieth Dynasty[?]), and Setau (TT288/9) and Anhotep (TT300, viceroys of Nubia under Rameses II).

Upstream, we have already noted Setau, high priest of Nekhbet at el-Kab (page 48, who would remain in office until at least Year 4 of Rameses IX), while downriver from Thebes we know of high priests of Seth at Ombos, of Osiris at Abydos, and of Onnuris at Thinis datable to the time of Rameses III.[99] At Heliopolis, Rameses III's son Meryatum B was certainly high priest under Rameses V,[100] and may originally have been appointed during his father's reign. Across the river at Memphis, the *Sem*-priesthood was held by Rameses III's son Khaemwaset E (cf. pages 16, 67, 69), but it is less than clear who held the Memphite high priesthood itself. A certain Pahemnetjer, perhaps a brother-in-law of vizier Hori I, had succeeded the latter's father, Hori A, around the end of the reign of Sethy II,[101] but a new man, Iyroy,[102] seems to have been appointed under Siptah: he was certainly in office during the reign of Tawosret. Whether he survived the transition to the Twentieth Dynasty is unknown: indeed, we subsequently have no clearly dated Memphite high priests until the middle of the Twenty-first Dynasty.[103] On the other hand, there is a Khaemwaset (Q) with the expansive titles of *Sem*-priest, Memphite high priest, mayor of Thebes, and vizier, known from a faience stela found at Memphis, who probably belongs to the Twentieth Dynasty on stylistic grounds.[104] But how he might relate to the aforementioned *Sem*-priest Khaemwaset (he lacks Khaemwaset E's title of King's Son) or the vizier of the name known under Rameses IX[105] is wholly obscure.[106]

Deir el-Medina

The village occupied by the artisans who undertook the construction of the royal tombs in the Valleys of the Kings and the Queens had been established back in the time of Thutmose I (fig. 49). By the reign of Rameses III, it had a long-standing organization, built around two teams of workmen—of the 'Left' and 'Right' sides, each with its own foreman, deputy, and scribe, under the overall management of the Scribe of the Tomb.[107]

There is a gap in our knowledge of the occupants of some of these senior posts at the beginning of Rameses's reign, and it is not until Year 11 that we find Wennefer v as Scribe of the Tomb, who was succeeded by Amennakhte v in Year 24, who remained in office until near the end of the reign of Rameses VI. On the other hand, we have a full series of foremen: on the Left, Anakhtu ii, Ipuy ii, Nekhemmut i, and Khonsu v; and on the Right, the long-serving Hay iv (from Year 1 of Amenmeses to Year 22 of Rameses III) and Inhurkhawy ii (who was in office until Year 4 of either Rameses VI or VII).

While their principal task was to build the king's tomb in the Valley of the Kings, the Deir el-Medina craftsmen were also deployed on other commissions, in particular tombs for the royal family. Surviving records include those of the completion of a tomb "of the King's Son" in Year 24,[108] work on the "eastern treasury" of the "Charioteer of Usermaatre-meryamun" (probably in Prince Prehirwenemef's QV42: see page 64, below) on Year 25,

FIGURE 49 Deir el-Medina, the village of the artisans responsible for the tombs in the Valley of the Kings.

I *prt* 7, and plastering in the "western chamber" of "the *Sem*-priest" (probably in Prince Khaemwaset's QV44) on the 22nd of the same month.[109]

The basis for life in the village was a monthly delivery of grain, which represented the pay of the workers and which could both be itself used for making bread and beer, and be traded for a wide range of goods and services.[110] However, problems with the regular delivery of grain to the community started to become apparent in the mid-20s of Rameses III's reign, an undated letter to the vizier To reporting that, while work was proceeding satisfactorily on tombs that had been commissioned for the royal children, the community was "utterly impoverished," with storehouses empty and a delivery of grain apparently reclaimed in exchange for a substandard batch.[111] Matters seem to have come to a head in Year 29: on II *3ḫt* 21 the Scribe of the Tomb Amennakhte denounced the fact that the grain ration was twenty days late and secured the issue of forty-six sacks of emmer wheat from the memorial temple of Horemheb two days later.[112] Interestingly, this issue coincided with To taking on the newly recombined vizierate (cf. page 50, above).

Nevertheless, shortfalls in deliveries continued, and a few months later, on II *prt* 10, with that month's rations eighteen days overdue (and those of the previous month apparently also lacking), the whole Deir el-Medina crew left the village and gathered at the back of the memorial temple of Thutmose III;[113] there, they were found by Amennakhte and the other senior members of the community. The following day they gathered at the southern gate of the Ramesseum, where the Scribe of the Right Pentaweret iii obtained some cakes for them; after spending the night there, they entered the temple enclosure on Day 12. At this, the chief of police Montjumose left to confer with the mayor, and after appealing to senior members of the temple staff, the outstanding rations for I *prt* were issued. The following day, the workmen returned to the entrance to the Deir el-Medina area, where Montjumose called on them to fetch their wives and children and follow him to the memorial temple of Sethy I; this further escalation resulted in the outstanding II *prt* supplies being provided on Day 17.

However, the following month a further strike took place, although on this occasion the complaint was over "evil being done in this place of Pharaoh"—clearly local corruption that may have been felt to be behind the repeated failures to maintain grain deliveries. These delays continued, only half-rations being issued at the very end of IV *prt*, the vizier sending a message to the effect that this was all that could be scraped together, given a general grain shortage. Our final view of these events comes with a further sit-down protest—this time at the memorial temple of Merenptah—on I *šmw* 13, the mayor of Thebes being harangued into giving a provisional issue of fifty sacks of emmer wheat. But the problem was clearly now endemic, and exacerbated by a parallel steady increase in the price of grain; while no strikes are known for Year 30, there is evidence for protests in both Years 31 and 32,[114] and the general malaise so demonstrated must have been an important contributor to the events that would unfold during the latter year (see pages 74–79, below).

3 THE FAMILY AND MURDER OF RAMESES III

The Royal Family

The Ramesside Period differed from earlier eras of Egyptian history in that, for the first time, male members of the royal family other than the king could appear on monuments by virtue of their birth rather than their political or sacerdotal titles.[1] Thus, under Sethy I, Crown Prince Rameses appeared more than once in his father's temple at Abydos while, after his own accession, his sons were depicted both in military tableaux and (with their sisters) in long processions that were a feature of many of Rameses II's temples.[2]

Like other decorative motifs of his earlier namesake, the 'procession of royal children' was adopted by Rameses III in his Medinet Habu memorial temple, as was their depiction in scenes of warfare, paying homage to their father, or on the back-supports of his statues. However, while in the case of Rameses II's family all images had been labeled with names and titles, those of Rameses III's offspring were carved with blanks left in their label texts where their names should have been (fig. 50). In some cases, the blank space was accompanied by generic titles (fig. 51), and in one very odd case two are given substantive titles, but the rest only generic ones—but still all with names left blank (pages 71–73, with fig. 65). Queens are also shown at Medinet Habu—but label texts are either wholly absent or the cartouche has been left blank (fig. 52).

The oddity of the situation is exacerbated by the fact that we *do* have tombs for royal sons completed and named during their father's reign. On the other hand, the two tombs belonging to ladies who are known to have been wives of Rameses III do not mention him anywhere, and seem to have been decorated entirely during the reigns of their sons.

FIGURE 50 Northern end of the procession of princes in the porch of the Second Court of the memorial temple of Rameses III, showing the last of the later-labeled images (that of [Rameses-]Meryamun; see further fig. 63) and the first of the never-named figures.

FIGURE 51 Officials labeled only with their titles in the First Court of the memorial temple, including eight King's Sons (distinguishable by their sidelocks).

The queens

On contemporary monuments of Rameses III, only one named wife is definitely shown, and then only once: Iset (D) Ta-Hemdjert, depicted on a statue of the king (fig. 24) in his temple of Mut at Karnak (fig. 54 left).[3] Hemdjert (with the alternate spelling, 'Hebnerdjent') appears to have been the mother of the queen (on the basis of her name, perhaps of foreign ancestry), the syllable 'Ta' meaning 'she of'. It seems also that Iset would on occasion abbreviate her name to that of her mother, especially after her husband's death. This seems to be indicated by a statue reinscribed by Rameses VI, known to have been Iset's son (see just below), on which his mother's damaged name should probably be read that way (fig. 54 right);[4] "Hemdjert" is also cited as the grandmother of Iset E, a known daughter of Rameses VI, in an inscription installing the younger Iset as God's Wife of Amun.[5]

Iset D's tomb in the Valley of the Queens (QV51)[6] was decorated in the name of Rameses VI, who gives her the title of King's Mother, confirming that he was indeed her son, as well as Lady of the Two Lands and Mistress of Upper and Lower Egypt, but *not* King's (Great) Wife, a lack that contributed to a long-running debate over whether Rameses VI was indeed a son of Rameses III, or actually a grandson (see further, just below).

FIGURE 52 Figure of the queen in the Festival of Min reliefs at Medinet Habu, with the titles of King's Great Wife, but no name ever inserted into her cartouche.

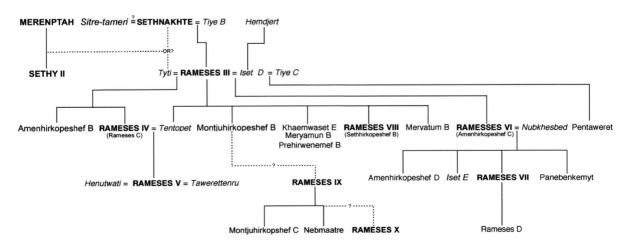

FIGURE 53 Reconstructed family tree of the Twentieth Dynasty. Broken lines indicate purely hypothetical relationships.

FIGURE 54 Queen Iset D: left, on the back-pillar of the west statue at the entrance to the South Temple of Rameses III at Karnak; right, on the back-pillar of a statuette of Rameses VI, usurped from Rameses IV (Luxor Museum CG42153).

The Valley of the Queens had been since the early Nineteenth Dynasty the preferred—but not exclusive[7]—burial place for royal wives (fig. 55). Iset D's tomb was of simple form, with an axial corridor leading to a burial chamber (containing a granite anthropoid coffin), with two subsidiary chambers. Decoration comprised predominantly the queen and deities. Next door to it (fig. 56) was cut a very similar sepulcher (QV52),[8] differing principally in having a third subsidiary room off the burial chamber; it was also decoratively very similar, in both composition and style.

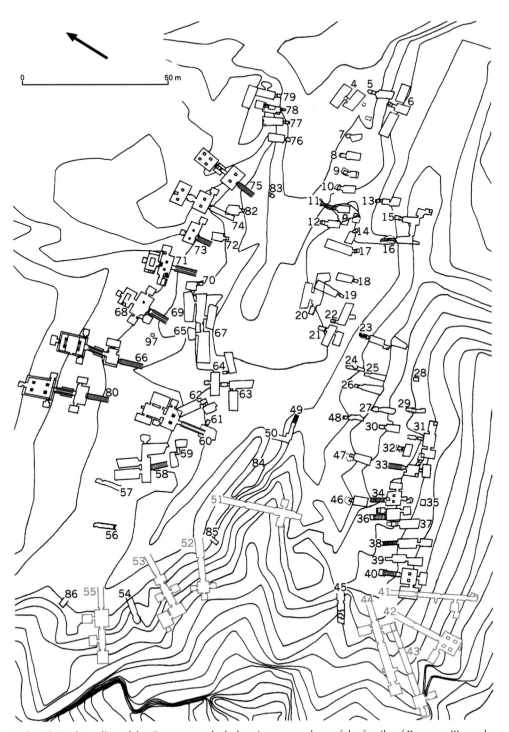

FIGURE 55 The Valley of the Queens; tombs belonging to members of the family of Rameses III are shown in red.

FIGURE 56 Western end of the Valley of the Queens, with the tombs of Tyti (QV52), Rameses C (QV53), and Amenhirkopeshef B (QV55); the tomb of Iset (QV51) is just out of shot to the left.

This belonged to a King's Daughter, King's Sister, King's Mother, King's Great Wife, Lady of the Two Lands, God's Wife, God's Mother, Mistress of Upper and Lower Egypt, Tyti (fig. 129). A curious feature of the tomb is that while most cartouches are carved, with no sign of usurpation, in some parts they have been inscribed in paint only, in contrast to the carved texts surrounding them (fig. 57). At present this is difficult to explain. Another oddity is that, while the tomb was explicitly "given by favor of the king," that king was nowhere named, and for many years Tyti was left in limbo as far as her historic position was concerned. Recent opinions varied from her being a spouse of Rameses III[9]—perhaps even a daughter-wife[10]—to her being perhaps a daughter of Rameses IX, wife of Rameses X, and mother of Rameses XI.[11]

The solution to the problem came when an old copy of a now-destroyed section of a papyrus dealing with the tomb robberies of the late Twentieth Dynasty (see, further, page 120, below) came to light, allowing us to read that a group of tomb robbers had opened "the tomb of the King's Wife Tyti of King Usermaatre-meryamun . . . ."—without doubt QV52. With this ancient statement of Tyti's affiliation, it is thus possible to definitively place her as a spouse of Rameses III.[12] Concerning the identity of Tyti's kingly father, her additional title of King's Sister would seem to confirm that he was Rameses III's own sire, Sethnakhte, although one cannot rule out Merenptah, making Tyti a sister of Sethy II if she were a child of Merenptah's old age. Given that Iset was the mother of Rameses VI, Tyti must have been the mother of one of the other two reigning sons of Rameses III—Rameses IV and Rameses VIII (on whom, see below); since the reign of Rameses VIII was extremely

FIGURE 57 Tyti before the Four Sons of Horus in the eastern side room of QV52.

brief, and came nearly three decades after the death of Rameses III, Rameses IV clearly seems the more likely candidate.

Thus, we have the situation that these two wives of Rameses III were both buried by their sons, without explicit mention of their husband. This is most curious and potentially suggestive, especially when taken with the blank queen's cartouche (and other blanks) at Medinet Habu. The circumstances under which we learn of a third wife, Tiye (C), further contribute to the feeling of unease as to the situation at Rameses III's court, given that she would end her life condemned for plotting the murder of her husband (see pages 74–77, below).

The children

In marked contrast to the situation in the sepulchers of his wives, Rameses III features heavily in the extant decoration of the tombs of his sons, accompanying their images throughout.[13] Most were in the Valley of the Queens (figs. 56, 58), but one was cut in the Valley of the Kings (KV3—fig. 6), although virtually nothing of its decoration survives, save the king's cartouches over the entrance and a few traces of figures in the first corridor.[14] It was of quite elaborate form, with a four-pillared hall and a number of subsidiary rooms, and is presumably the prince's tomb mentioned as being begun in the Valley in Year 28 (see, further, p. 70, below).[15]

FIGURE 58 The southwest section of the Valley of the Queens, with the tombs of 'Pentaweret' (?, QV41), Prehirwenemef B (QV42), Sethhirkopeshef C (QV43), and Khaemwaset E (QV44).

Of the Valley of the Queens tombs, three had been either taken over from an earlier occupant, or had been at least begun for an earlier owner. Of them, QV42 was ultimately occupied by the First King's Son of His Person, Charioteer of the Great Stable, Prehirwenemef (B).[16] As noted above (page 16), Rameses III gave all his sons names previously borne by senior sons of Rameses II, and often even the same functional titles, and this was the case with Prehirwenemef, named for Rameses II's third son.[17] His other title indicates that he was a first-born son by one of Rameses III's wives, but there are no clues as to which one. QV42 had been originally quarried for a queen, whose figure is in one case still visible on the wall, unfortunately without any trace of her identity, although the figure has similarities with those in QV52, suggesting a date late in the Nineteenth Dynasty. The sarcophagus had also been made for a woman, with her name and titles all erased (fig. 59).

On architectural grounds (a steep staircase leading down to the entrance, in contrast to the gentle slope found in tombs definitely of the Twentieth Dynasty), QV55[18] was at least begun in the Nineteenth Dynasty. However, the inner parts are consistent with tombs created under Rameses III, with tableaux of the king and the tomb's owner (fig. 60, top), the King's Son and Master of Horse, Amenhirkopeshef (B)—one of two sons

FIGURE 59 The granite coffin appropriated, along with QV42, for Prehirwenemef B (Turin S5435).

of that name born to Rameses III (see below).[19] While his mother is nowhere named, Amenhirkhopeshef is stated to have been "born of the God's Wife, God's Mother and King's Great Wife," paralleling Tyti's titles so closely that he may with some confidence be called her son. A rough anthropoid granite coffin was provided (fig. 60, bottom), of relatively small size, suggesting that the prince died young—something consistent with a subsequent son of Rameses III being given the same name.

Adjacent to QV55, and of similar plan, was cut QV53,[20] which today is in a much poorer condition and almost devoid of decoration, albeit with traces of two phases of application, suggesting again that the tomb had been appropriated. However, one fragment preserves the text "[…] born of the [King's] Great Wife, the [King's] Son, Rameses," while another, now gone, included Rameses III's prenomen; other fragments indicate an overall decorative scheme similar to that found in other tombs of the king's sons. The simple name "Rameses"[21] suggests that the tomb's owner was the future King Rameses IV, who generally employed this as his nomen, contrasting with other kings of the Twentieth Dynasty, who compounded "Rameses" with another personal name.

The remaining tombs of Rameses III's sons in the Valley of the Queens lay close to QV42 (fig. 58). They were all cut to the same basic plan, with a gently sloping main axis, a narrow burial chamber at the end, and one or two side chambers. QV41[22] is devoid of surviving decoration, although it may have at one time been plastered, with the decoration removed. It has been speculated that it may have belonged to the subsequently disgraced prince dubbed "Pentaweret" (see pages 74–76, below).[23]

Both the others, however, preserve decoration, very similar to that in QV55, and in QV43[24] naming the King's Son and First Charioteer, Sethhirkopeshef.[25] QV44[26] belonged to the First King's Son and *Sem*-Priest of Ptah, (Rameses)-Khaemwaset (E) (fig. 61), his titles marking him out as the first-born son of one of the queens, and second in the priestly hierarchy at Memphis. An enhanced status for Khaemwaset might be suggested by the fact that, rather than the anthropoid granite coffins given to Amenhirkopeshef and Queen Iset, he was given a fully-fledged sarcophagus (fig. 62), with his recumbent figure on the lid, as provided for kings since the time of Merenptah, and also used for Rameses III himself (see pages 109–15, below).

FIGURE 61 Rameses III and Khaemwaset in QV44.

FIGURE 62 Upper part of the lid of the sarcophagus of Khaemwaset, from QV44 (Turin S5215).

Alongside the evidence provided by these tombs are the names later added to the pair of processions of princes and princesses carved as mirror images on either side of the axis of the colonnade at the rear of the Second Court at Medinet Habu. As already noted, names and titles had been omitted when the scenes were carved under Rameses III; however, after his death, a number of the princes' images had names and titles added (fig. 63), although none of the princesses ever received names. The history of these additions, and their implication, were the subject of a long drawn-out debate which, however, seems now essentially settled.[27] Thus, it appears most likely that under

| 1. Rameses C | 2. Amenhirkopeshef C | 3. Amenhirkopeshef | 4. Sethhirkopeshef B | 5. |
| RAMESES IV | RAMESES VI (prenomen) | RAMESES VI (nomen) | RAMESES VIII (prenomen) | |

FIGURE 63 The princes in the procession in the northern half of the portico of the Second Court in the memorial temple of Rameses III, to which names and titles were added under Rameses IV and Rameses VI.

Rameses IV the first figure in each procession was labeled "Fanbearer on the King's Right, Executive (*iry-p't*—often equivalent to Crown Prince),[28] Generalissimo, King's Son of his Body, his beloved, Rameses," with the name in a cartouche. This would thus appear to be Rameses IV marking the figure as himself, with his princely titles, but with the cartouche to which he was now entitled as king; the rest of the figures remained unlabeled for the time being.

Another example of such princely titles combined with the simple name "Rameses" in a cartouche is to be found in TT148, belonging to the Third Prophet of Amun, Amenemopet, where Prince Rameses is shown appointing the latter to office under Rameses III.[29] This tomb seems to have been decorated only under Rameses IV, but contains various scenes looking back to the reign of his father, including one explicitly dated to his Year 27.

Back at the Medinet Habu procession, following his accession on the death of his nephew Rameses V, Rameses VI followed a similar approach to his elder brother by quoting his own princely titles, but with a king's cartouche. However, rather than just using his nomen, as had Rameses IV, he took over two princely figures, thus allowing him to display both his prenomen (with part of his princely titles) and nomen (with the rest).[30] Thus, the second figures are called "Fanbearer on the King's Right, Executive, King's Scribe, King's Son of his Body, his beloved, Nebmaatre-meryamun," and the third "Fanbearer on the King's Right, King's Scribe, Master of Horse, King's Son of his Body, his beloved, Rameses-Amenhirkopeshef-netjerheqaiun." Rameses VI then labeled the next seven figures for the King's Son and Master of Horse (&c) Sethhirkopeshef; the King's Son and First Charioteer Prehirwenemef; the King's Son and First Charioteer Montjuhirkopeshef;[31] the King's Son and high priest of Re-Atum Meryatum;[32] the King's Son and *Sem*-priest of Ptah Khaemwaset; the King's Son Amenhirkopeshef; and the King's Son Meryamun.[33] The remaining princely figures were left unlabeled.

ʜef B   6. Montjuhirkopeshef B   7. Meryatum B   8. Khaemwaset E   9. Amenhirkopeshef B   10. Meryamun B

The primacy of Sethhirkopeshef in the order would seem to reflect that he was the one brother still alive under Rameses VI, as he would later become king as Rameses VIII. This is made clear by the addition, following his accession, of kingly cartouches to the figures labeled for Sethhirkopeshef, the northern receiving his prenomen, Usermaatre-Akhenamun, the southern his nomen, Rameses-Sethhirkopeshef-meryamun.

Comparing the names at Medinet Habu with those known from the Valley of the Queens, there is a clear 1:1 correlation between the Prehirwenemefs and Khaemwasets. There are, however, two Amenhirkopeshefs at Medinet Habu, and only one in the Valley of the Queens, but given the evidence of the size of the coffin in the latter, the hypothesis that he had died young, and that a later-born brother received his name (and title)—and later became Rameses VI—seems quite reasonable. While there is only one Sethhirkopeshef at Medinet Habu and one in the Valley of the Queens, some have queried whether they were both the same person, or whether there were two—a prince who died young (QV43) and one who lived on to become Rameses VIII.[34]

In this connection, tomb KV19 in the Valley of the Kings[35] was originally "granted as a royal favor" for a King's Son, King's Scribe, Generalissimo, Rameses-Sethhirkopeshef[36]—almost certainly none other than the future Rameses VIII—which has been used as an argument for two sons of Rameses III named Sethhirkopeshef. However, since the Medinet Habu procession shows two Amenhirkopeshefs where there were indeed two princes of the name, the single Sethhirkopeshef at Medinet Habu would point to there having only ever been one. As for the two tombs, the most likely solution would seem to be that he acquired the second later in his career, perhaps during the last years of Rameses III, or perhaps better under his brother Rameses VI or nephew Rameses VII. Under the latter option, this could have been a recognition of Sethhirkopeshef's status as the senior surviving prince of his generation by replacing his 'juvenile' tomb in the Valley of the Queens with a new one. Given that we have no tomb for Rameses VIII, it has been suggested that it may have been intended that it be continued as his kingly tomb, but was soon abandoned on the king's early demise. KV19 was then appropriated for Montjuhirkopeshef C, a son of Rameses IX, the Seth-animal in the one text sketched out for Sethhirkopeshef being erased and replaced by an image of Montju.

Of the sons listed at Medinet Habu, but without known tombs in the Valley of the Queens, one must presumably have been the owner of KV3 (unless disgraced prior to the reign of Rameses VI, and thus excluded from the labeling at Medinet Habu). Amenhirkopeshef C lacks a princely tomb, and seems to have been the second-ranking royal son by the latter part of the reign (cf. next page), and might thus be a good candidate. Montjuhirkopeshef may have been the prince of that name who was buried in tomb KV13, originally constructed for the chancellor Bay before his disgrace and execution.[37]

The tomb was taken over under Rameses VI for his son, Amenhirkopeshef D, but a Prince Montjuhirkopeshef had his sarcophagus placed in the corridor outside Amenhirkopshef's chamber.[38] One option is that he was another son of Rameses VI, named after his uncle, but it is also possible that he was the brother of Rameses VI of that name—although his placement after the presumably long-dead Prehirwenemef in the Medinet Habu procession might suggest that Montjuhirkopeshef was also dead before Rameses VI came to label the Medinet Habu processions.[39]

Outside the Medinet Habu lists, the other cases of names being filled into spaces originally carved blank are restricted to two princes—Rameses and Amenhirkopeshef C, the future Rameses IV and VI. Their names were added to the images of the two princes shown taking part in the Festival of Min in the peristyle of the Karnak bark temple (fig. 64), in which case it is possible that the addition was made during Rameses III's lifetime since, if added during Rameses IV's reign, one would have expected the use of a cartouche as in the Medinet Habu lists (and also in TT148). This would suggest that during the latter part of the reign, the senior living sons were the eldest of each of the two Great Wives. Since Amenhirkopeshef C had been born during Rameses III's reign, 'replacing' Amenhirkopeshef B, it would seem to follow that Sethhirkopeshef was also relatively late-born—unless the order of birth *by each* wife was the determining factor—in which case he could have been older, but borne by Tyti. This would, however, be contrary to the situation seen under Rameses II, who also maintained multiple Great Wives, but for whom seniority in the succession was apparently determined wholly by overall order of birth. Rameses C's name is also found inserted in the label text of a spectator in a linear tableau of ceremonial games under the Window of Appearances at Medinet Habu (fig. 85),[40] and also in certainly contemporary attestations in a graffito in the temple of Amenhotep III at Soleb in Upper Nubia,[41] on a lintel where he is depicted before his father,[42] and on a loose block once seen at Medinet Habu.[43] There seems to be but one example of another prince depicted and labeled in a primary context under Rameses III: Prehirwenemef, on the back-pillar of a statue of the king from the Mut-precinct at Karnak.[44]

Noted above was a case where, although the majority of anonymous princes were given only generic titles, two, each leading a row, were given substantive ones (fig. 65). Both were given the titles of King's Scribe and Generalissimo, but the upper one was defined as leading infantry, with the additional title of Executive, and the lower as leading bowmen, and also called Fanbearer on the King's Right. The former seems likely to have been intended to be Rameses C,[45] although why, having inserted a specific person's titles, their name was omitted is almost impossible to explain. The lower set of titles do not correspond to those of any known son of Rameses III,[46] suggesting that the prince in question could have fallen into disgrace before the filling-in of names in the Medinet Habu procession under Rameses VI. One option is that he was the person later referred to as "Pentaweret" but it is possible

FIGURE 64 Princes Rameses C and Amenhirkopeshef C in the company of their father; west wall of peristyle court, Karnak bark temple.

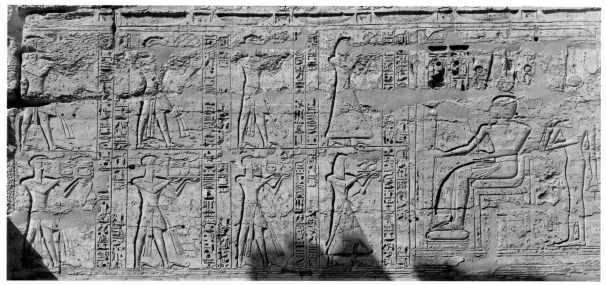

FIGURE 65 Princes offering to Rameses III on the west wall of chapel 3, on the north side of the First Hypostyle Hall in the king's memorial temple. All except the leading prince of each row have only generic princely titles.

that other princes may also have suffered a fall from grace (cf. the question of the owner of KV3, above).

A similar situation is found in part of the Festival of Min sequence of reliefs in the Second Court at Medinet Habu. Here (fig. 89), princes are among the carriers of the king's throne litter, and the area above these figures was marked out for text columns giving their names and titles. However, only the first two columns were ever filled in, giving the titles "Fanbearer on the King's Right Hand, Executive, Royal Scribe, Generalissimo, Senior <King's Son> of his body, his beloved"—the titles of an heir to the throne, presumably, implicitly, Rameses C—but with a blank where the name should have been.

In contrast to the quantity of material—even if in many cases distinctly equivocal—relating to the sons of Rameses III, almost nothing is known of his daughters: none of their images at Medinet Habu were ever labeled (fig. 66). The sole potential daughter is the God's Adoratrix Tentopet,[47] depicted in the Rameses III/IV section of the Khonsu temple at Karnak (fig. 67), who may be same person who became the King's Great Wife, Lady of the Two Lands, King's Mother, (Dua)tentopet, owner of QV74 in the Valley of the Queens.[48] In spite of the latter's apparent lack of a King's Daughter title (except for one possible amended example in QV74), many adoratrices were daughters of a king,[49] with Rameses III probably the best candidate for the father in this case. (Dua)tentopet has generally been assessed as later the wife of Rameses IV and mother of Rameses V, although no unequivocal evidence has yet come to light.[50]

FIGURE 66 Princesses at the extreme northern end of the portico of the Second Court in the memorial temple; none of the reliefs intended to represent daughters of Rameses III were ever given label texts.

Murder

Apparently absent from the monumental sources for the family of Rameses III are his wife Tiye C, and a son later referred to as "Pentaweret." However, both were key actors in a series of papyri (or sections of what was once a single papyrus—fig. 68) written at the beginning of the reign of Rameses IV—dealing with the assassination of Rameses III himself.[51]

The documentation comprises a series of reports on the individuals accused, together with a consolidated record of the final proceedings. Unfortunately, significant parts are missing, through both accidental damage and the activities of the original finders who cut the document(s) into sections for subsequent sale; in addition, part (pRifaud) only survives in a poor nineteenth-century copy, the actual fragments having become lost in the interim.

From the preamble to the main record, it is clear that the investigation was nominally initiated by Rameses III himself. He is recorded as appointing a panel of a dozen officials, headed by two senior Treasury officers, supported in particular by a team of butlers,[52] to investigate and impose punishment, without reference back to him. For many years it was thus surmised that the king had actually survived the conspiracy, although dying soon afterward. However, more recent examination of the king's body has shown that his injuries were such—a deeply gashed throat—that his death would have been instantaneous (see page 148, below). Accordingly, the decision to place the process under the late king's auspices may have been taken for political reasons—perhaps to establish the new king, Rameses IV, as wholly 'above' the proceedings, or simply a view that a reign only formally ended with the king's burial.

The events originated in the *ipt nswt*—the part of the royal establishment concerned with the king's family, and often translated into English by using the Ottoman Turkish term 'harem,' although it was certainly a very different institution from this.[53] Plots emerging from it can be traced back to the Old Kingdom,[54] with the question of which of a king's male offspring should succeed to the throne clearly a potential trigger for intrigue.

Insofar as a formal mechanism for succession is concerned, circumstantial evidence implies that the heir to the throne should be the eldest son of the king (ideally by his Great Wife), who would at some point be formally proclaimed heir, and would eventually carry out his father's burial as the final filial act of a dutiful son. Since most kings had but one Great Wife at any one time, the heir apparent would have been clear, assuming that she did indeed have a son.

Rameses II had multiple Great Wives, with an inherent potential for conflict, but this seems to have been avoided by adopting strict order of birth as the basis for seniority, a seniority made concrete in the stereotyped processions of royal children that were included in many of the king's temples.[55]

FIGURE 67 The Adoratrix Tentopet, probably a daughter of Rameses III, wife of Rameses IV, and mother of Rameses V, as shown in the temple of Khonsu at Karnak.

Thus, we find that the first, third, ninth, eleventh, and sixteenth sons were the offspring of Queen Nefertiry, and the second, fourth, and thirteenth (the eventual successor, Merenptah) were those of Queen Isetneferet.

In contrast, as already noted, the processions incorporated into the monuments of Rameses III never had names added during his reign, suggesting that there was a lack of consensus as to each son's relative placement in the order of seniority—and thus succession to the throne. Likewise, the failure to label queenly images also suggests issues with deciding which lady was appropriate to the context in question—again, contrasting with the situation under Rameses II. Coupled with the economic malaise suggested by the Deir el-Medina strikes during Years 29, 31, and 32, the last of these years may well thus have seen both broader dissatisfaction with the current regime and increasing dispute over the succession, especially as the king aged. Historically, such circumstances have been regular catalysts for revolutions and coups d'état. And thus they probably proved in the days leading up to II *šmw* 15 of Year 32 of Rameses III's reign.[56]

The object of the coup was to place a Prince "Pentaweret" on the throne instead of Prince Rameses C, who would seem to have been Rameses III's own nominee. Like many other accused named in the documents, "Pentaweret" was not charged under his own name, although in this case it was not a specially formulated negative one, as was bestowed on many of the other accused. The account of his examination runs as follows:

> Pentaweret, the one who was given this other name.
>
> He was brought in because of his having colluded with Tiye, his mother, when she had plotted the matters with the women of the harem, raising rebellion against his lord.
>
> He was set before the butlers, to be examined; they found him guilty; they left him where he was, and he killed himself.[57]

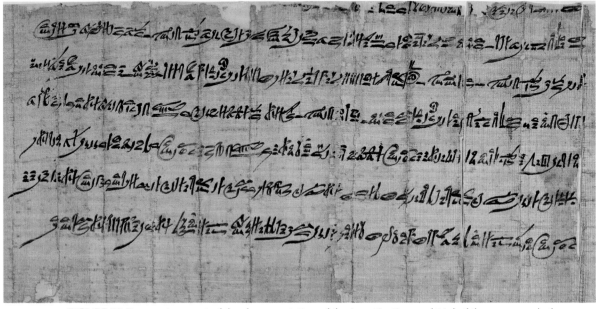

FIGURE 68 Papyrus Lee, part of the documentation of the investigation and trial of those accused of culpability in the assassination of Rameses III (Pierpoint Morgan Library, New York, Amh Egy Pap 51).

The fact that the prince was allowed to commit suicide suggests that it was recognized that he had been, to some extent at least, a puppet of his mother and her co-conspirators. Indeed, he lacks the epithet of "great criminal" given to most of the accused, and is grouped with offenders of the third level, whose crimes were principally failing to report the conspiracy, rather than active participation.

Tiye herself, and the other female members of the harem, are not included in the extant documentation: one assumes that they were dealt with by a separate panel, whose records are currently lost. On the other hand, wives of some men who had been part of the plot were tried alongside their husbands, six being executed.

Of Tiye's male associates in the conspiracy, the leading figure seems to have been the man who heads the list of first-rank accused:

> The great criminal, "Paibekkamen," who had been a chief of a department.
>
> He was brought in because of his having been in collusion with Tiye and the women of the harem. He made common cause with them, and had begun to take messages out to their mothers and brothers who were there, saying: "Stir up the people! Incite enmity!," to raise rebellion against their lord.[58]

He was examined by the senior members of the court, who, having found him guilty, "caused his punishment to befall him"—clearly a euphemism for execution. That Paibekkamen was the linchpin of the conspiracy is made clear by his being explicitly named in a number of subsequent indictments, alongside a butler, "Mesudsure," who was apparently his right-hand man.

An important participant was "Binemwaset," a troop commander of Kush, and a senior figure in the viceregal regime, who had been incited to participate by his sister, one of the harem 'retinue.' An ability to make use of Nubian troops would have been extremely useful to the conspirators; indeed, it was via this route that Amenmeses had probably been able to successfully revolt against Sethy II only a few decades before.[59] Another likewise key conspirator is likely to have been the general Payis, condemned to take his own life.

While most active conspirators were executed, some, like Pentaweret, were allowed to kill themselves rather than suffer execution (perhaps in some cases as a privilege of rank), including a general, a number of senior priests, a butler, and two scribes of the House of Life (an institution of learning). On the other hand, nine of those tried for failing to report what was going on rather than actually "raising rebellion" were executed, although most convicted of 'omission' rather than commission were allowed to kill themselves.

As well as incitement to rebellion by words, it appears that Paibekkamen also turned to magic:

He (a person whose name is seemingly lost) began to make magical writings for banishing and confusing, to make some gods of wax, and some people for causing people's limbs to be feeble. These were handed over to Paibekkamen … (and to) the other great criminals.[60]

While it has been argued that this passage is actually about manipulating people's feelings and actions, rather than voodoo-like use of wax dolls for black magic,[61] the wording seems very clear: given Egyptian beliefs in the reality of magic, it would not be at all surprising if the conspirators attempted to bolster their efforts through supernatural means. Certainly, the person involved was required to commit suicide.

The final group to be tried by the commission included some of their own members, "punished by cutting off their noses and ears, because they had abandoned the good instructions given to them. The women had gone and reached them at the place where they were. They had made beer-hall there with them and with (the condemned general) Payis."[62] Those so condemned for disorderly fraternization with a key defendant were the chief of police Nanayu and the soldier Tayinakhtethe, plus two judges, the scribe Maya, and the butler Pabes, the latter of whom committed suicide soon after his mutilation. Another judge, the standard-bearer Hori, although convicted of being "as one" with the participants, escaped with a harsh reprimand.

We thus have considerable detail as to the people involved in the conspiracy, and from their backgrounds can infer something of its strategy: the assassination of the king, followed by agitation against the succession of Prince Rameses C and the installation of Pentaweret with military support, possibly including some from Nubia. However, the location and details of the actual murder of the king are less clear.

That it occurred at Thebes is likely in view of the recovery of the related documents there: had it taken place in the north (for example, at Per-Rameses), it is unlikely that a copy of the records would have ended up in the southern city. A clue lies in the date of the death of Rameses III: at the beginning of the month during which occurred the Beautiful Feast of the Valley.[63] This was one of the key celebrations of the Theban ritual year, in which the king would normally be a participant.

As a primarily West Theban event, during which the bark of Amun visited the primary sanctuaries on that side of the Nile—including Medinet Habu—it would have made sense for the king to stay there. His obvious base would have been the palace buildings attached to his Medinet Habu memorial temple: the ceremonial palace itself

FIGURE 69 The Eastern High Gate of Rameses III's complex at Medinet Habu, from the southeast.

on the south side of the first courtyard of the temple, and the rooms in the Eastern High Gate (fig. 69), decorated with scenes of the king at leisure (fig. 70), which seems to have served as the king's private lodging. It may have been here—or perhaps in the more remote, now-destroyed, Western High Gate, which probably played a similar role[64]—that the king's life was brought to an end.

Whatever the follow-up plans for preventing the accession of Prince Rameses, these were clearly unsuccessful, as he was proclaimed king to the Deir el-Medina workforce on the sixteenth, by which time the tribunal to try the conspirators was already being established in the name of the late king. Nevertheless, the new Rameses IV was clearly keen to cement his status, burying his father on I 3ḫt 24,[65] exactly seventy days after his death (apparently the ritual minimum, to judge from the later statements of Herodotus), since the act of burial confirmed the officiant's status as legal successor.[66]

Rameses IV also commissioned the monumental document now known as the Great Harris Papyrus, and already referred to as a key source for the reign of Rameses III. Produced to the highest standards, with superb calligraphy and vignettes, it extended

FIGURE 70 Scene from the upper rooms of the Eastern High Gate, showing Rameses III with two young women.

over 117 pages, spread across a forty-meter scroll, and provided a comprehensive retrospective overview of the king's reign. It was divided into seven sections, the first being an introduction, after which sections II, III, and IV described in great detail the donations made by the king to the gods and temples at, respectively, Thebes, Memphis, and Heliopolis. The sections were separated by full-page vignettes of the king before the divine triad of the immediately following section (fig. 71).

Section V provided similar, yet more concise, data for the lesser temples of Egypt, with section VI giving a consolidated summary of all Rameses's gifts to the gods. Finally, section VII was devoted to a narrative presentation of the king's secular career, beginning with his dynasty's origins (page 6, above), running through his accession, activities abroad and at home, and ending with his final message to the world, put into his mouth by Rameses IV, commending the latter to his subjects as a final confirmation of his legitimacy and the confounding of the conspirators:

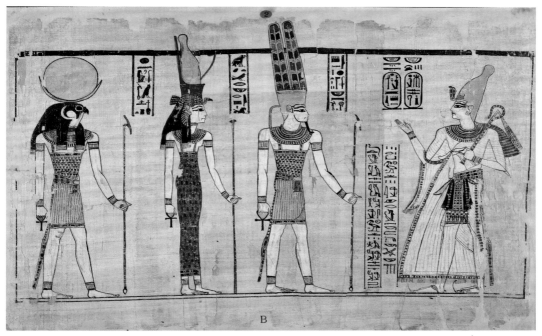

FIGURE 71 Rameses III before the Theban triad, as shown in the Great Harris Papyrus (pBM EA9999,2).

See, I have gone to rest in the Beyond, like (my) father Re, I have mingled with the great gods in heaven, earth and the Beyond. Amun-Re has established my son on my throne; he has taken my office in peace, as ruler of the Two Lands, sitting on the throne of Horus as lord of the two shores. He has assumed the *atef*-crown, like Tatenen, as Usermaatre-setepnamun, LPH, eldest son of Re, the self-engendered, Rameses-heqamaat-meryamun, the child, son of Amun, who came forth from his limbs, shining as Lord of the Two Lands; he is like a true son, praised for his father's sake. Attach yourselves to his sandals, kiss the earth in his presence, bow down to him, follow him at all times, adore him, praise him, magnify his beauty as you do to Re every morning. Present to him your tribute (in) his august palace, bring to him the gifts of the lands and foreign countries. Be zealous for his commissions, the commands which are spoken among you. Obey his orders, that you may prosper under him. Labor for him as one man in every work; drag for him monuments, dig for him canals, do for him the work of your hands, that you may enjoy his favor, in possession of his provision every day. Amun has decreed to him his reign upon earth; he has doubled to him his lifetime more than any king: the Dual King, Lord of the Two Lands; Usermaatre-Setepenamun, LPH, Son of Re, Lord of Appearances, Rameses-heqamaat-meryamun, LPH, given life forever.

FIGURE 72 Map of Thebes.

4 THE MANSION OF MILLIONS OF YEARS AND THE HOUSE OF ETERNITY

The Memorial Temple of Rameses III

Since the beginning of Egyptian history, the ideal Egyptian tomb had comprised two distinct elements: an accessible offering place where the worlds of the living and the dead met, and where sustenance and prayers could be delivered as part of a mortuary cult; and the actual burial place, usually subterranean, and intended to be sealed for eternity.[1] By the time of Rameses III, the kingly implementation of this scheme comprised a memorial temple (or "mansion of millions of years") close to the edge of the desert at Thebes West (figs. 72, 73), and a subterranean tomb in a desert wadi—now known as the Valley of the Kings (figs. 6, 74)—beyond the curtain of cliffs that rose behind the royal memorial temples.[2]

Although built to serve a dead king's funerary cult, these memorial temples differed from the mortuary temples of the Old and Middle Kingdoms in that the royal cult, rather than standing alone, was subordinated to those of the gods Amun and Re. Thus, the sanctuary on the main axis of the temple was that of a form of Amun specific to the temple in question. To its north was an open-court altar dedicated to the sun god Re, and to its south the shrine of the dead king and, until the Nineteenth Dynasty, a subsidiary sanctuary dedicated to his or her father.

While Eighteenth Dynasty examples had layouts that diverged significantly from those of contemporary cult temples, by the Nineteenth Dynasty they had become much closer to contemporary divine cult temples, albeit retaining the tripartite inner division.

FIGURE 73 The Theban necropolis in the 1960s, showing the royal memorial temples along the desert edge, the private tomb-chapels on the low hills beyond, with the Valley of the Kings behind the curtain of cliffs behind Deir el-Bahari at the top right. Medinet Habu lies just off the left-hand edge of the photograph.

FIGURE 74 The Valley of the Kings, showing the location of the two tombs datable to the reign of Rameses III.

Those of Sethy I and Rameses II (the Ramesseum) are relatively well preserved, although those of Merenptah, Siptah, and Tawosret (perhaps usurped by Sethnakhte) are reduced to their foundations (and that of Sethy II never identified).

The Ramesseum (fig. 75) provided a model for the memorial temple of Rameses III (figs. 76, 77),[3] although the latter was some 23 percent bigger. Today the best preserved of all New Kingdom memorial temples, the good condition of Rameses III's monument derives in part from its having become the headquarters of the Theban necropolis during the latter part of the New Kingdom, thus avoiding the dismantlement suffered by many others (cf. pages 24–25). Much later it was at the core of a Coptic community.

Rameses III's complex was erected close to the late–Eighteenth Dynasty memorial temple of Ay and Horemheb at Medinet Habu, and directly adjacent to a mid-Eighteenth Dynasty temple to Amun, which was enclosed within the new mudbrick wall erected as part of Rameses III's project. This wall included two unique High Gates, one to the east and one to the west, which incorporated features of Syrian *migdol* fortresses (figs. 69, 78, 131).

The western one is largely destroyed, but the eastern example, while denuded of most of its extensive mudbrick flanking elements, retains most of its stone structure. This was externally adorned principally with images, in raised relief, of the king smiting his enemies (fig. 78), while the rooms within its upper parts, most of which seem to have comprised royal lodgings, were decorated with scenes of the king and his womenfolk engaged in leisure activities (fig. 70).

FIGURE 75 The Ramesseum, memorial temple of Rameses II, model for Rameses III's memorial temple, and a venue for the protests of the latter's Year 29.

FIGURE 76
Medinet Habu.

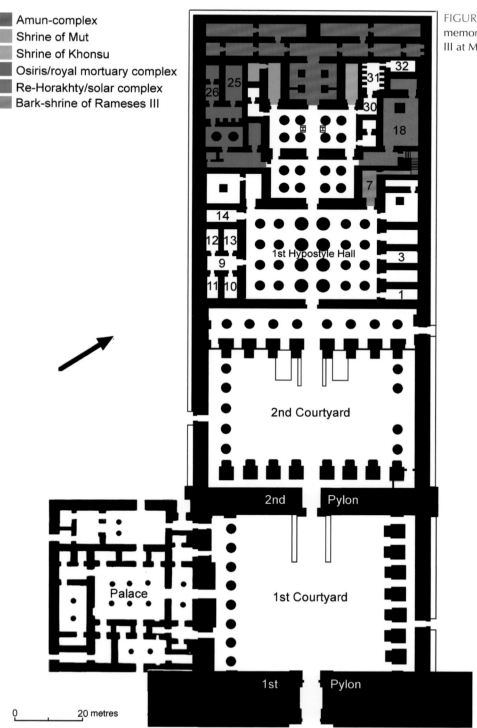

Amun-complex
Shrine of Mut
Shrine of Khonsu
Osiris/royal mortuary complex
Re-Horakhty/solar complex
Bark-shrine of Rameses III

FIGURE 77 Plan of the memorial temple of Rameses III at Medinet Habu.

1st Hypostyle Hall

2nd Courtyard

2nd   Pylon

Palace

1st Courtyard

1st   Pylon

0   20 metres

The memorial temple itself was fronted by a First Pylon bearing smiting scenes in sunk relief (fig. 79). Complementing these, the exterior walls of the temple were devoted to the king's physical prowess, either on the hunting field or in battle, and his generosity to the gods. Their sequence began on the rear wall of the building, with a Nubian campaign (page 46, fig. 43, above), continuing on the northern walls with depictions of Rameses's Second Libyan and Sea Peoples campaigns (pages 38–44, above; figs. 37, 38, 41). The decoration of the southern exterior of the temple (fig. 80) started at the First Pylon with a series of scenes of the king hunting antelope, wild donkeys, and bulls (fig. 81). Then, covering almost the whole length of the temple, was a vast festival calendar, listing the various daily feasts and services celebrated in the temple, together with the offering involved on each occasion (figs. 82, 83).

FIGURE 79 The First Pylon of the memorial temple.

FIGURE 80 View of the temple from the southeast.

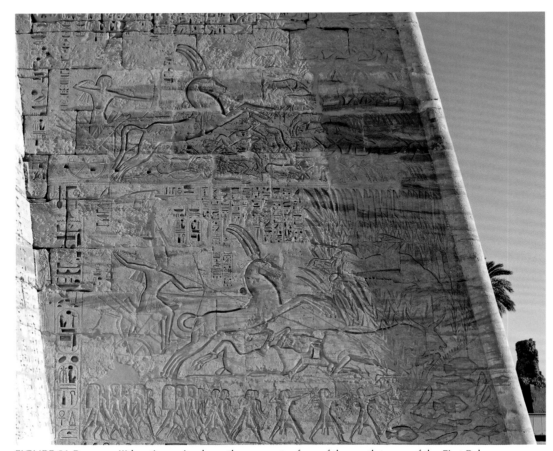

FIGURE 81 Rameses III hunting animals on the rear outer face of the south tower of the First Pylon.

A palace, a feature introduced to memorial temples at the beginning of the Nineteenth Dynasty, abutted the southern wall of the First Court, and was linked to it by a Window of Appearances (figs. 84 and 85). The palace had been built in two phases, the first based on the palace at the Ramesseum, its walls primarily of mud brick with various architectural features in stone. Its reconstruction in the second building phase changed the plan considerably, making the whole structure more complex. The roles of most of the various rooms are unclear, as is the degree to which it was ever a 'real' palace and how far it had an eternal role in accommodating the king's spirit when it posthumously attended events at the temple.

Within the First Court, the southern range was made up of columns, and the northern of seven piers, each fronted by a colossal statue of the king (fig. 86). The decoration of the court featured the celebratory aftermath of battles depicted on the exterior of the temple, along with those referring to festivals that took place in the temple.

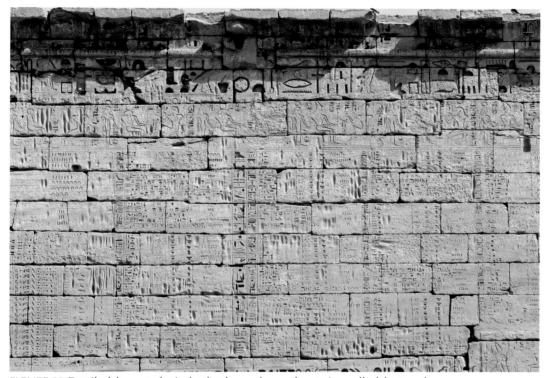

FIGURE 82 Detail of the great festival calendar on the south exterior wall of the temple.

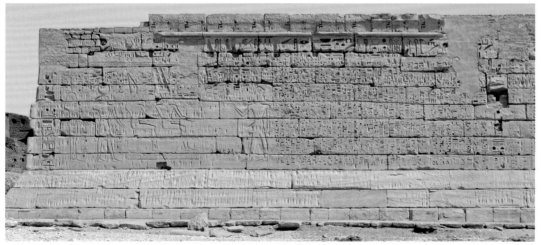

FIGURE 83 The western end of the south wall, showing the king before the gods.

FIGURE 84 The palace, built against the south side of the First Court, and communicating with it via the Window of Appearances.

FIGURE 85 The Window of Appearances, as seen from the First Court.

FIGURE 86 Northeast corner of the First Court.

FIGURE 87 The Second Pylon, with the presentation of Peleset, Denyen, and Shekelesh captives to Amun and Mut on the southern (left) tower, and the principal narrative of the Sea Peoples campaign on the northern.

FIGURE 88 The southwest corner of the Second Court, with the portico, adorned with largely missing sheathed figures of the king, on the right.

The Second Pylon bore texts and scenes relating to the Sea Peoples campaign (fig. 87), the Second Court to which it gave access being colonnaded on all four sides (figs. 88, 118). Its decoration was split between, on the south side, scenes relating to the First Libyan War (fig. 36) and, on the north, religious festivals, in particular that of the god Min (fig. 89).

The portico on the west side of the court was fronted by two rows of pillars, the outermost originally bearing engaged figures of the king, depicted as though sheathed in linen (so-called Osirid statues). The upper parts of its walls were decorated with scenes taken from the royal coronation ritual, but the lower sections contained mirror-image processions of the king's children on either side of the doorway leading into the First Hypostyle Hall (figs. 50, 63). As noted in chapter 3, these figures, and others in the temple, were not given name labels during the original decorative process.

Beyond the two open courts were a series of hypostyle halls, now denuded down to the lowest drums of their supporting columns (fig. 90). The First Hypostyle Hall had a series of small shrines along its northern side, at least some of which served as chapels

FIGURE 89 The king emerging from his palace, carried by his sons and other dignitaries, to take part in the Festival of Min; the label texts above the leading carriers were never completed (see p. 73, above). North side of the Second Court.

FIGURE 90 The denuded remains of the hypostyle halls of Rameses III's memorial temple, with the vestiges of the chapels of the Theban triad beyond.

to the various gods, with two (rooms 1 and 7) apparently devoted to the living king. On the south side was the temple treasury (rooms 9–13), and just to the east of this a chapel dedicated to the king's hero, Rameses II (14).

The much smaller Second Hypostyle Hall—on the parallel of the corresponding part of the Ramesseum, perhaps originally adorned with an astronomical ceiling—gave access to the three principal cult complexes of the temple: of Amun, Mut, and Khonsu (center); Re-Horakhty (north: fig. 91); and the dead king, fused with Osiris (south). The latter complex differed from the earlier surviving examples (those of Hatshepsut and Sethy I) in making no explicit provision for the king's father. It was also much more extensive than earlier such complexes, and incorporated, apparently for the first time, extracts from the Book of the Dead (fig. 92). An astronomical ceiling was also provided in the innermost sanctuary (room 25), which had on its end wall a stela that acted as the ultimate focus for the cult of the dead king, marking the liminal point between the worlds of the living and the dead (fig. 93).

The solar complex of Re-Horakhty included a largely open area (room 18), incorporating a solar altar, as well as a now-destroyed roof terrace, accessed via a stairway. Also largely destroyed is the central complex of the Theban trinity, accessed via the

FIGURE 91 The open court of the solar complex of the temple, which contained an altar to the sun.

FIGURE 92 North wall of room 26, part of the Osiris/ royal mortuary complex, adorned with scenes of the Fields of Iaru from Chapter 110 of the Book of the Dead.

FIGURE 93 The inner shrine (room 25) of the Osiris/royal mortuary complex, with a double false door at its western end, showing Osiris receiving the homage of the king, who fused with him in death.

Third Hypostyle Hall, which has side chapels apparently dedicated to aspects of Horus, and a complex associated with an ennead of deities headed by a primordial form of Amun (rooms 30–32). Amun's main cult complex was flanked by shrines of his wife, Mut, and son, Khonsu, with a four-pillared bark shrine and a room directly beyond whose decoration included a large double false-door stela (only the lowermost part of which survives). Flanking this were further rooms whose exact purpose is obscure, but which clearly had roles to play in the daily cult of the god.

The area outside the temple proper was occupied by a wide range of subsidiary structures, the inner enclosure wall accommodating storerooms and workshops, although a garden seems to have been maintained directly west of the palace. Beyond the inner enclosure wall lay offices and houses for the temple personnel. These were expanded later in the Twentieth Dynasty, when the former Deir el-Medina community was transferred to within the outer walls of the Medinet Habu complex.

The Tomb of Rameses III

As already noted (pages 8–13), Sethnakhte's tomb, KV11, was unfinished at his death and the king was buried in the usurped sepulcher of his predecessor, Tawosret. The construction of KV11 was continued by Rameses III, resulting in one of the largest tombs in the Valley of the Kings (figs. 6, 7, 94), with a total length of 188 meters, exceeded only by Hatshepsut's KV20 and Sethy I's KV17. All the cartouches in the portion of the tomb already decorated by Sethnakhte were replaced by those of Rameses, either by recarving or by simply being filled with plaster and painted (for example, fig. 101, left-hand scene).

Sethy I had been the first king to produce a tomb decorated from the entrance to the very innermost chambers,[4] the wall decoration beginning with a scene of the king being welcomed by Re-Horakhty. This was then followed by the text of the Litany of Re, which occupied the first corridor. This scheme was adopted by his successors, Siptah's KV47[5] interposing kneeling, winged figures of Maat between the king/Re-Horakhty tableau and the actual entrance gate. KV11 followed this approach, the text of the Litany occupying corridor B and the associated images the upper parts of walls of corridor C (figs. 95, 96, 97).

Rameses III's takeover of the tomb included the addition of a series of side chambers to corridors B and C, resulting in the destruction of some existing elements of the Litany of Re in B, and the Hours 1–3 of the Book of *Amduat* that occupied the lower walls of C.[6] Substitute texts were added to the doorjambs of, and in corridor B also inside, the new rooms.[7] The first pair of new side chambers, opening off corridor B and each originally fitted with a single-leafed door, were adorned with images of bakers, cooks, butchers, and leatherworkers (Ba—fig. 98a), and sailing boats (Bb—fig. 98b).

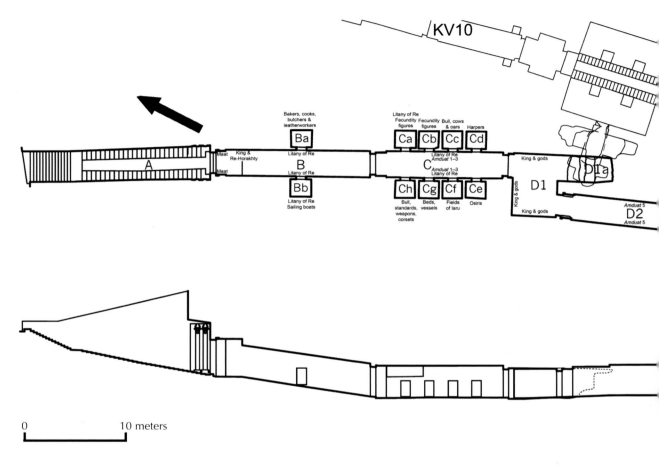

FIGURE 94 Plan and section of KV11.

The eight rooms accessed from corridor C had an eclectic mix of images: fecundity figures (Ca, Cb—figs. 98c, 99a);[8] a sacred bull, cows, and oars (Cc—fig. 99b); harpers before deities (Cd—fig. 122); Osiris (Ce—fig. 99c); the Fields of Iaru (Cf—fig. 100a); beds and vessels (including Aegean Late Helladic IIIC pottery: Cg—fig. 100b); and a bull, standards, weapons, and armor (Ch—fig. 100c). It has been reported that each room gave access to a shaft,[9] but no such feature has been identified by modern survey work.[10]

This range of motifs is unknown elsewhere in the Valley of the Kings, and adequate explanation for the full ensemble has thus far eluded researchers.[11] On the other hand, the Fields of Iaru appear again deeper in KV11 (see below), and also, as previously noted, in the memorial temple of Rameses III himself (fig. 92). Also elsewhere in KV11,

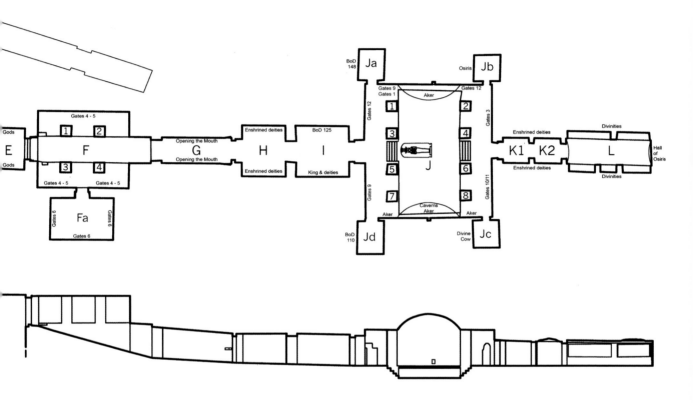

in chamber I, is a copy of the Negative Confession, like the Fields of Iaru a feature of the Book of the Dead (BD125), a composition not previously extensively used in kingly tombs. The Book of the Dead described and enabled the passage of the mortal individual to immortality, in contrast to the divine king, whose posthumous destiny had hitherto been aided by separate corpora of texts. These had begun with the Old Kingdom Pyramid Texts and during the New Kingdom were represented by the so-called 'Books of the Underworld,' built around the nocturnal voyage and rebirth of the sun god.[12] During the first part of the Eighteenth Dynasty, these had begun with the Book of *Amduat*, with additional compositions, in particular the Book of Gates, coming into use at the end of that dynasty; yet more evolved during the Nineteenth Dynasty.

FIGURE 95 Re-Horakhty greets the king on the east (left) wall of corridor B of KV11.

FIGURE 96 Looking down corridor C toward the truncated corridor D1a, in a photograph from the 1960s. High-level niches are visible just inside the doorway, as are the entrances to the eight side chambers, added when the tomb was taken over by Rameses III.

Apart from an isolated early example,[13] these works remained exclusive to kings until the Third Intermediate Period, with very little of the Book of the Dead leaking in the other direction, the main exceptions being particular Book of the Dead spells found on royal funerary equipment, and the adoption of the composition's Opening of the Mouth sequence from Sethy I onward. In this context, the inclusion of certain major elements of the Book of the Dead in both the tomb of Rameses III and his memorial temple is somewhat surprising. Insofar as can be judged from their generally unfinished or truncated nature, no later kingly tombs include such features until the Twenty-second Dynasty, when Osorkon II, in his tomb at Tanis, went beyond even Rameses III by being depicted having his heart actually weighed, rather than simply including the generic image of the Judgment Hall that formed part of the Book of Gates.[14]

FIGURE 97 Corridor C is decorated with the Litany of Re, the text in vertical columns, with its divine images shown in the high-level niches; this is the one in the east wall. Visible below is the entrance to chamber Ca, and the way that its cutting removed part of the text of the Litany, the missing parts of which were recarved in the thicknesses of the new doorways.

FIGURE 98 Details of the decorations of side-chambers: a. Ba; b. Bb; c. Ca.

FIGURE 99 Details of the decorations of side chambers: (top) Cb; (middle) Cc; (bottom) Ce.

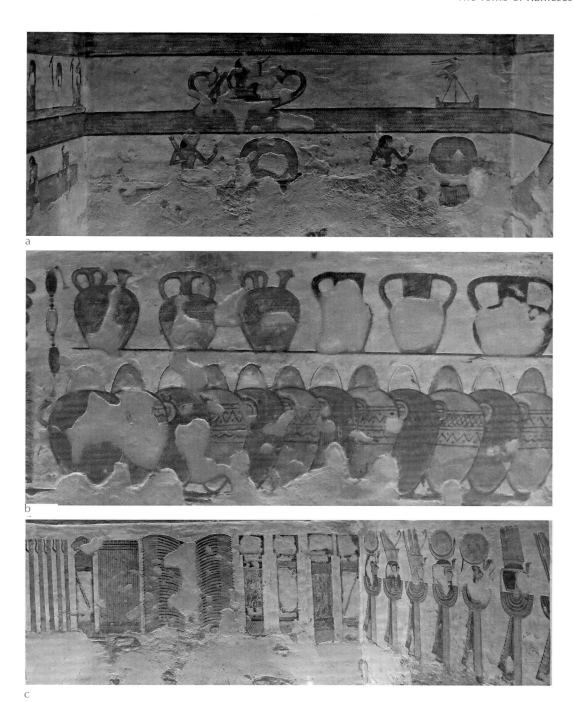

FIGURE 100 Details of the decorations of side chambers: a. Cf; b. Cg; c. Ch.

FIGURE 101 The east wall of chamber D1, showing the king (originally Sethnakhte, with the names changed to those of Rameses III, added in paint in the left-hand scene and carved in the right) offering to Atum (left) and Ptah (right).

Beyond corridors B and C, the original scheme of Sethnakhte was retained unaltered, apart from the royal cartouches (figs. 11, 101), and when further new work was undertaken by Rameses III, in corridor D2, this was conventionally adorned with the *Amduat* (Hour 5: fig. 102). Well-room E then received images of deities (fig. 103), and upper hall F the Book of Gates (Hours 4 and 5) and the shrine of Osiris, as had been the case in this part of the tomb since the time of Sethy I. The Book of Gates continued, with Hour 6, in the hall's annex, Fa (fig. 104).

A revived feature, apparently last seen in the tomb of Rameses II (KV7), was the placement of the Opening of the Mouth ritual in corridor G, which then led to a pair of antechambers (H and I), primarily adorned with images of divinities (fig. 105). From here onward the tomb is now badly damaged, as a result of flooding during the nineteenth century AD (see page 143–44, below).

Beyond lay the burial chamber (J: figs. 106, 107, 108a, b, 125, 126), with a central transverse crypt of the type introduced into royal tomb architecture under Rameses II, replacing the end crypt used between Amenhotep II (KV35) and Sethy I. Unlike in the tombs of Merenptah, Siptah, and Tawosret/Sethnakhte, where the sarcophagus was placed across the axis of the tomb, that of Ramses III was placed along it, an orientation maintained in subsequent sepulchers of Twentieth Dynasty kings.[15]

FIGURE 102 The east wall of corridor D2, adorned with Hour 5 of the Book of *Amduat.*

Although the majority of the decoration of the burial chamber was taken from the Book of Gates, the room also contained scenes from the Book of the Earth (or *Aker*), introduced in Merenptah's KV8. The side chambers contained a variety of decorative elements, including depictions of the Fields of Iaru (Jd) and the Book of the Divine Cow (Jc: fig. 108c). Various depictions of deities were placed on the walls of the rooms (K1, K2, and L) directly beyond the burial chamber, culminating in a depiction of the Hall of Osiris at the extreme end of the tomb (fig. 109).

Kingly stone sarcophagi had become cartouche-shaped under Thutmose III, and with the exception of the late–Eighteenth Dynasty examples of Akhenaten, Tutankhamun, Ay, and Horemheb, had continued to be of that form down to Rameses III.[16] Under Merenptah, a recumbent figure of the osirid king had been added to the upper surface of the lid, and that of Rameses III (fig. 110) followed this pattern. However, while Merenptah's coffers had been adorned with schemes based on the Book of Gates, a wholly new one had been adopted for the examples of Siptah and Tawosret (usurped for Sethnakhte, fig. 14)—

FIGURE 103 View from the end of corridor D2, showing the western of its two niches, well chamber E, and the upper hall F, with the descending ramp into the innermost parts of the tomb.

FIGURE 104 Chamber Fa, cut on the west side of upper hall F, adorned with Hour 6 of the Book of Gates.

FIGURE 105 Chamber H, with most of its decoration, mainly comprising images of enshrined deities, destroyed by flood water.

FIGURE 106 The southern end of the ruined burial chamber J, looking toward the innermost rooms, K1, K2, and L.

FIGURE 107 Detail of the decoration of the east wall of the burial chamber, as drawn by the Franco-Tuscan expedition during 1828–29.

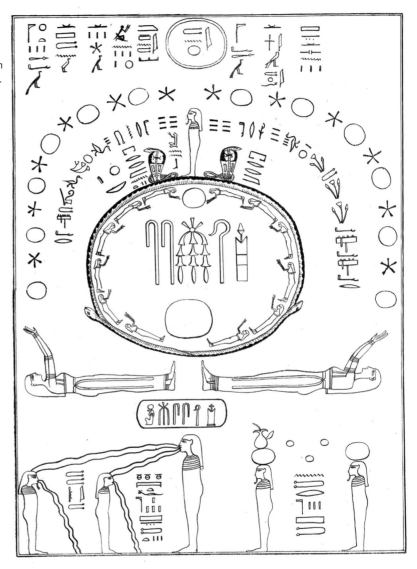

which would also be used on that of Rameses IV. Curiously, however, the coffer of the sarcophagus of Rameses III (fig. 111)[17] reverted to Merenptah's Gates-based approach—albeit decorated *inside* with the Siptah/Tawosret/Rameses IV scheme.[18]

The arrangement of scepters on Rameses III's recumbent figure on the lid also followed the earlier king, rather than his immediate predecessors and successors. Accordingly, although no traces of recarving can be seen in the royal names on the sarcophagus, it is possible that it may have been begun for Sethy II, whose unfinished tomb lacks an outer sarcophagus (and even space for one),[19] and then continued for Amenmeses,[20] before

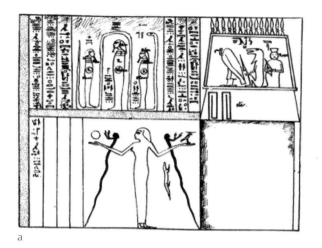

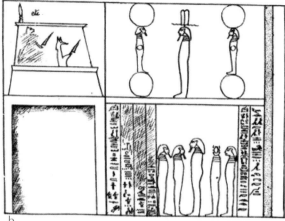

FIGURE 108 Sketches made by Eugène Lefébure during the early 1880s of now largely lost elements of the decoration of rear portions of KV11: a. detail of the decoration of the southern end of the east wall of the burial chamber, with the entrance to chamber Jb; b. detail of the decoration of the southern end of the west wall of the burial chamber, with the entrance to chamber Jc; c. rear wall of chamber Jc.

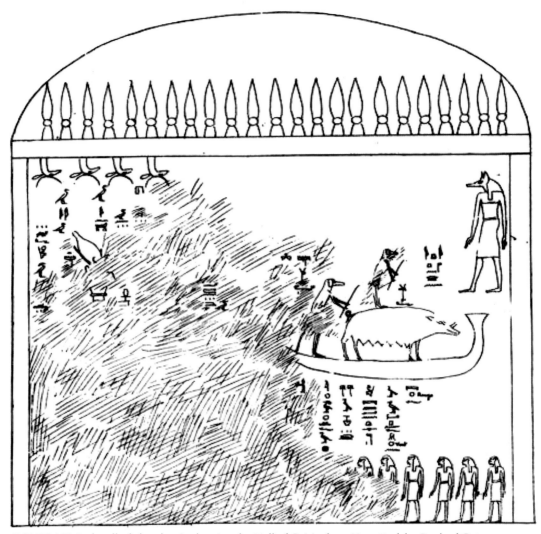

FIGURE 109 End wall of chamber L, showing the Hall of Osiris, from Hour 5 of the Book of Gates.

finally being used for Rameses III. Curiously, fragments of the lid of a second, somewhat smaller, granite sarcophagus have come to light in the burial chamber, in the well, and in the adjacent tomb KV10. It is unclear whether this might have come from the interment of a second individual (a wife or child?) in KV11, or is intrusive.[21]

Of the remainder of the king's funerary equipment, the trough of his innermost coffin, carved out of a log of cedar wood and once extensively gilded and inlaid (fig. 112), was ultimately reused for the reburial of Amenhotep III in the cache of royal mummies in the tomb of Amenhotep II (KV35), closed with a lid bearing name of Sethy II.[22] To

FIGURE 110 Lid of the sarcophagus of Rameses III, with an image of the king flanked by Isis, Nephthys, and snake deities on the upper surface. Underneath is carved a figure of Isis, rather than Nut who is usually found under the lid of a coffin or sarcophagus (Fitzwilliam E.1.1823).

judge from the burials of Merenptah and Siptah, it is likely that a calcite outer coffin was also employed, and a number of potential fragments have been found in the Valley of the Kings that might belong to this.[23] Nothing is known of any canopic equipment belonging to Rameses III, and thus it is unclear whether he followed Siptah in having an 'integral' calcite chest, of the kind employed since the time of Amenhotep II,[24] or giant individual jars of the type used by Rameses IV.[25]

FIGURE 111 Coffer of the sarcophagus of Rameses III, its exterior sides decorated with extracts from the Book of *Amduat*, the head end with an image of Nephthys, its foot with Isis, and its interior with sections from the Book of Gates in a scheme also found on the exteriors of the coffers of Siptah, Tawosret/ Sethnakhte, and Rameses IV (Louvre D.1).

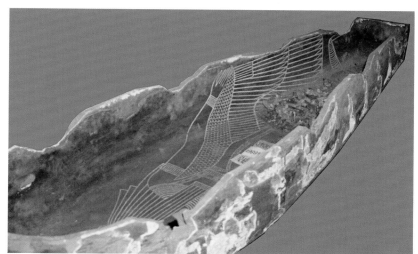

FIGURE 112 The trough of the inner coffin of Rameses III, carved from a single log of cedar and originally gilded and inlaid, with the original painted image of the winged Nut on its floor. The piece was found in KV35, holding the mummy of Amenhotep III, and closed by a lid bearing the name of Sethy II (Cairo CG61040).

a   b   c   d

FIGURE 113 Shabtis of Rameses III: a. OIM E10755; b. Louvre AF425; c. Louvre N656B; d. BM EA67816 (top), EA8695 (bottom).

Otherwise, of the king's funerary equipment, only a handful of shabtis are known (fig. 113).[26] Surviving examples are of a range of types and materials, ranging from wood (one),[27] to calcite (four),[28] to bronze (five).[29] The latter material had been hitherto rare for shabtis, although an example is known for Rameses II, and would later be used for Pasebkhanut I and at least one contemporary.[30] From the example of earlier and later kingly tombs, one would have expected KV11 to have contained wooden figures of deities,[31] and probably a pair of life-size wooden so-called guardian statues[32] at the entrance to the burial chamber, but no traces appear to have been found, and the nineteenth-century AD flooding of the tomb is likely to have contributed to the destruction of any wooden material that might have remained.

5 LIMBO

The troubled and tragic end of the reign of Rameses III boded ill for the prospects of his successors. Rameses IV's issue of pHarris I was clearly intended to provide not only an expansive eulogy for his late father, but also a means for the new king to illuminate himself in reflected glory. A conscious presentation of himself as a legitimate king *par excellence* (unsurprising in light of the circumstances of his accession) may be seen in his use of the epithet *m3'ty*—'the one of Maat'—in his most widely used nomen cartouche. This was accompanied by a desire to make a mark both with building (beginning a memorial temple one-and-a-half times larger than that of his father)[1] and longevity (praying for a lifespan to rival that of Rameses II).[2]

Sadly, Rameses IV was granted a reign of only six years; his son Rameses V only four. The latter seemingly left no son, as the throne then passed back up a generation to Amenhirkopeshef C (Rameses VI), another son of Rameses III (fig. 114). He is the last New Kingdom king of whom we have substantive evidence for activity in the Levant, in the form of a statue base at Megiddo.[3] Rameses VI's son and successor, Rameses VII, was also followed by yet another son of Rameses III, Sethhirkopeshef (Rameses VIII), presumably after the premature death of his only known son, Rameses D, although the brevity of the reign of Rameses VIII could potentially suggest some form of extended power struggle.

The origins of the next king, Rameses IX, remain unclear, although it has been suggested that he was a grandson of Rameses III, via Montjuhirkopeshef B.[4] His reign saw a further deterioration in Egypt's position, with, around its end, civil conflict that culminated in the 'suppression' of the high priest of Amun, a "year of hyenas," an apparent division of the kingship, and a premature end to the reign of his successor, Rameses X.[5] Rameses IX's tenure also saw the beginning of a rash of tomb robbery at Western Thebes, which was the subject of a series of investigations and trials.[6]

FIGURE 114 Statue of Rameses VI frog-marching a captive; from Karnak (Luxor Museum CG42152).

Among their records we read that in Year 1 of the *wḥm-mswt*, the 'Renaissance' era that was established following the temporary reunification of the country during the latter years of Rameses XI, "Pawer, a workman of the Necropolis, . . . showed [a group of robbers led by herdsman Bukhaef] the tomb of the King's Wife Hebdjert" (that is, Iset D). Bukhaef claimed that the tomb was already open when they reached it, whereupon the gang "brought away an anthropoid coffin of silver and a mummy-board of gold and silver."[7] Not only this, Bukhaef was also implicated when one "Pawerkhetef . . . had [a group of robbers] open the tomb of the King's Wife Tyti of King Usermaatre-meryamun, LPH, with him leading us, and we took that anthropoid coffin of gold and silver."[8] Thus, within a bare few decades of their interment, both queens had been turned out of their coffins, and possibly their mummies destroyed as well.

Even the kings' tombs in the Valley of the Kings were falling victim to this wave of robbery, the earliest known intrusion during this period being into the sepulcher of Rameses VI (KV9), which had various textiles and metal vessels removed, probably before II *prt* 14 of Year 9 of Rameses IX.[9] Although this pilfering was much less serious than the treatment meted out to the two queens less than a decade and a half later, it is clear that the stripping of the kings' tombs was not long delayed.

Thus, six years after Iset and Tyti had been tumbled out of their coffins, dockets on the coffins that currently sheltered the now-restored mummies of Sethy I and Rameses II, dated to Year 6 of the *wḥm-mswt*, show that these kings had recently received the attentions of plunderers. Two decades later, Rameses III himself had become a victim—although not necessarily for the first time—his outer wrappings being replaced as part of an 'Osirification' carried out in Year 13 of Nesibanebdjedet I (figs. 115, 127c). It may have been at this point that he parted company with his own coffin (cf. page 114, above), and was placed in a simple coffin of red-painted cartonnage (fig. 127a).[10] It has been suggested that some part of this restoration may have involved material known to have

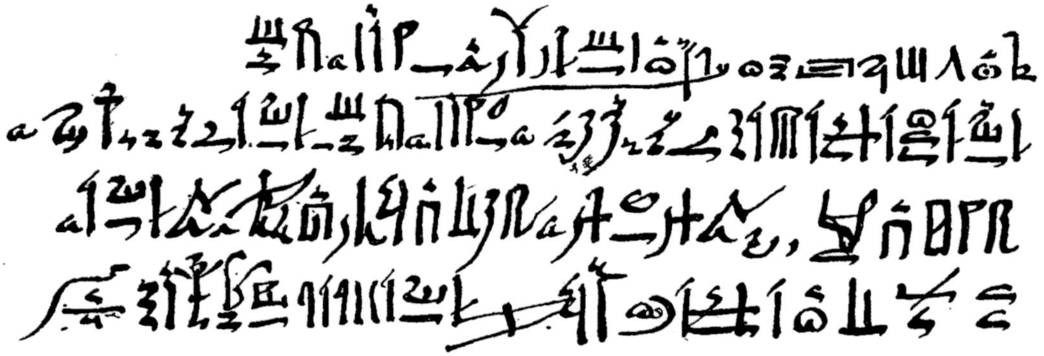

FIGURE 115 Docket on the mummy of Rameses III:
Year 13, II šmw 27. The day when the First Prophet of Amun-Re-nesunetjeru Panedjem, son of the First Prophet of Amun Piankh, sent the Scribe of the Temple Djeserusukhonsu and the Scribe of the Tomb Butehamun to Osirify King Usermaatre-meryamun, in order that he remains and endures forever.

been stored in KV49, an unfinished Eighteenth Dynasty corridor tomb, about fifty meters from KV11,[11] and in which a glass ring bearing the king's prenomen was found in 2018.[12]

Unlike some kings, the peregrinations of whose remains can be traced in detail via successive dockets on their mummies,[13] nothing is known of the location of Rameses III's mummy subsequent to its restoration under Nesibanebjedet I: whether it was returned to KV11 or moved to another tomb, perhaps grouped with others, as was the case with Rameses I, Sethy I, and Rameses II, is unknown. In any case, however, the mummy of Rameses III ultimately came to rest in a tomb just south of Deir el-Bahari (TT320—fig. 116), which seems originally to have belonged to Queen Ahmes-Nefertiry of the early Eighteenth Dynasty.[14] Much later, it had been taken over for the Twenty-first Dynasty high priest of Amun Panedjem II and his family, and it was some time after the burial of the last of the latter, probably during the second decade of the reign of Shoshenq I,[15] that some thirty displaced mummies of royalty and their households were placed in the tomb.[16] For some reason, the encoffined mummy of Rameses III ended up inside the colossal outer coffin of Ahmes-Nefertiry (fig. 117):[17] it would remain there for three millennia.

Of Rameses III's monuments, at least some of his various cult temples probably remained in regular use for some time after his death, especially as, in the reduced economic circumstances of the Third Intermediate Period, resources will have been scarce for any replacement. On the other hand, the temple at Edfu was dismantled during the latter part of the Ptolemaic Period, when a new temple of Horus was constructed at right angles to the more ancient sanctuary, the forecourt of the vast new temple overlying its site.

In contrast to most memorial temples, which fell into disuse within a few years of their authors' demise, and subsequently fell victim to stone robbery, Rameses III's

FIGURE 116 Western Thebes, showing Sheikh Abd el-Qurna, the Khokha, Asasif, and Deir el-Bahari, with the location of TT320 indicated.

Medinet Habu edifice survived largely intact. This owed much to it being part of a wider complex, including the Small Temple, which continued to be part of the Theban processional ceremonial and was the object of restoration and extension in Twenty-fifth Dynasty, Ptolemaic, and Roman times. The precinct became the headquarters of the Theban necropolis administration later in the Twentieth Dynasty and, as already noted, also the location of the workmen's community from Deir el-Medina, as its security was increasingly threatened by bandits infiltrating from the Western Desert.[18] It seems to have been here in the precincts of Medinet Habu that many of the royal mummies—probably including Rameses III himself—were restored following robbery and prior to reburial.

Although there is little evidence for the memorial temple's use during the Third Intermediate Period, the area in front of it would become a high-status cemetery, housing at least one king's tomb (Horsieset I, of the mid-ninth century), and those of the Twenty-fifth/sixth Dynasty God's Wives of Amun. The associated town grew through Ptolemaic times, with massive expansion in Roman times of what was now regularly referred to by the name Djeme.[19]

Following the departure of the king's mummy, KV11 seems to have been simply abandoned. Certainly, it was accessible in classical times, containing two short Demotic graffiti plus some twenty in Greek,[20] extending from the entrance to corridor D2, with two Greek and one Demotic text in room Cc. However, this falls far below the huge numbers found in some other sepulchers,[21] in particular the nearby KV9 (Rameses VI). This might suggest that KV11 may have been more difficult to access (cf. the lack of graffiti beyond corridor D2)—or simply perceived as less interesting by ancient tourists: KV9 was believed to be the tomb of the legendary Memnon.[22] Nor does KV11 have evidence of the presence of Coptic monks, as did Rameses IV's KV2, with its many Coptic inscriptions, and its immediately surrounding area, including KV3, which had been transformed into a Christian chapel. This may have been owing to KV2 and KV3's location close to the entrance of the Valley of the Kings, and also the shallow descent and roominess of KV2 as compared with many earlier tombs in the Valley.

Christianity also appropriated parts of the Medinet Habu complex, the "Holy Church of Djeme" being erected in the Second Court (fig. 118) at the core of the still-flourishing settlement of Djeme, which by the seventh/eighth centuries AD had a population of between one thousand and two thousand people.[23] However, by AD 800 the town had been abandoned, and the site would remain uninhabited until modern times.

FIGURE 117 The colossal outer coffin of Ahmes-Nefertiry, within which was found a further coffin containing the mummy of Rameses III; from TT320 (Cairo CG61003).

FIGURE 118 The remains of the church in the Second Court of the memorial temple at Medinet Habu, seen in 1858.

6 Resurrection

The Tomb of the Harper

With the coming of Islam in the seventh century AD, the ancient monuments of Egypt become enveloped in shadow.[1] Among them were the tombs of the Valley of the Kings, which only begin to re-emerge with the first visits by westerners during the late seventeenth and early eighteenth centuries. Among them was Richard Pococke (1704–65, fig. 119),[2] who was in Egypt during 1737–38, and produced an illustrated book on his travels. This included a highly schematic view of the Valley of the Kings (fig. 120), a sketch map (fig. 121, bottom), and a number of plans of tombs in the Valley. These included KV3 and those of Rameses III and Amenmeses (fig. 121, top); regarding the latter pair, Pococke comments that "[a]t the entrance of K. a large bull's head is cut in relief, and by a hole mark'd k. at the further end of it, there is a communication with L."[3] It is unclear whether the "bull's head" is the example in the opening tableau of the Litany of Re, or singling out one of the bovid-headed pilasters at the entrance (fig. 10).

The plan showing the conjoined tombs is interesting in that it is reversed, with KV10 shown to the right of KV11, rather than left (although the tombs are shown the right way around in Pococke's view of the Valley); it also shows KV11 only as far as D1a. It is unclear whether the latter was owing to an interrupted visit or whether this was due to some

FIGURE 119 Richard Pococke, by Jean-Étienne Liotard (Musée d'art et d'histoire, Geneva, inv. 1948-22).

FIGURE 120 The Valley of the Kings, as drawn by Richard Pococke. His tombs can be identified as follows:

A. KV1 (Rameses VII).

B. KV2 (Rameses IV) [plan misattributed to A].

C. KV7 (Rameses II).

D. KV8 (Merenptah) [wrongly noted as "Stopped up": plan misattributed to B].

E. KV9 (Rameses VI) [wrongly noted as "Stopped up": plan misattributed to C].

F. "Stopped up": probably KV12.

G. KV13 (Bay).

H. KV14 (Tawosret/Sethnakhte) [plan misattributed to G].

I. KV15 (Sethy II) [plan misattributed to H].

K. KV11 (Rameses III).

L. KV10 (Amenmeses).

M. KV18 (Rameses X).

N. KV6 (Rameses IX).

O. KV3 (son of Rameses III) [plan misattributed to N].

difficulty in proceeding further, although the rear chambers were certainly accessible to James Bruce thirty years later; rooms Ba and Bb are also missing from the plan. There are also inaccuracies in the plan of KV3 (as in most of the rest of Pococke's plans). Pococke was also "desirous, if possible, to see the temple of Medinet-Habou, which the Sheik's son seem'd to promise me; but I found these two governors of the neighbouring villages were not friends."[4] He thus had to depart without having seen Rameses III's principal West Theban monument.

The next recorded visit to the tomb of Rameses III comes in 1769, with the arrival of James Bruce (1730–94: fig. 122),[5] while en route to investigate the origins of the Nile.

The beginning of his visit to the Valley is recorded as follows:

> About half a mile north of El Gourni, are the
> magnificent, stupendous sepulchres, of Thebes. The
> mountains of the Thebaid come close behind the
> town; they are not run in upon one another like ridges,
> but stand insulated upon their bases; so that you can
> get round each of them. A hundred of these, it is said,
> are excavated into sepulchral, and a variety of other
> apartments. I went through several of them with
> a great deal of fatigue. It is a solitary place; and my
> guides, either from a natural impatience and distaste
> that these people have at such employments, or, that
> their fears of the banditti that live in the caverns of the
> mountains were real, importuned me to return to the
> boat, even before I had begun my search, or got into
> the mountains where are the many large apartments
> of which I was in quest.
>
> In the first one of these I entered is the prodigious
> sarcophagus, some say of Menes, others of Osimandyas;
> possibly of neither. It is sixteen feet high, ten long, and
> six broad, of one piece of red-granite; and, as such,
> is, I suppose, the finest vase in the world. Its cover, is
> still upon it, broken on one side, and it has a figure in
> relief on the outside. It is not probably the tomb of
> Osimandyas, because, Diodorus says, that it was ten
> stadia from the tomb of the kings; whereas this is one
> among them.[6]

Since this passage is immediately followed by the
description of what is certainly the tomb of Rameses III,
this would at first sight seem to indicate that the lid of the
sarcophagus in that sepulcher was still in place on the coffer
at the time of Bruce's visit, and that the damage to the lid was
caused by robbers attempting to access the interior. However,
it was certainly no longer in place at the end of the century
(see page 131, below), and in 1818 Giovanni Belzoni (1778–

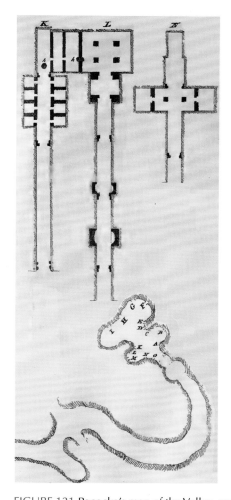

FIGURE 121 Pococke's map of the Valley, and
plans of his tombs K and L. The chambers
flanking the second corridor of K make it
clear that this is KV11, while its juncture
with L, and the general plan of the latter,
indicate that this is KV10, but the relative
positions of the two have been reversed. The
plan labeled N is KV3 (although the map's
tomb N is actually Rameses IX's KV6), but
the second pair of columns has been omitted
from the main chamber, and the right-hand
side room misplaced. However, in spite of
their inaccuracies and confusion over their
placement, Pococke's plans are all most
creditable, given the conditions and time
constraints under which he was working.

FIGURE 122 James Bruce (engraving by S. Freeman from a painting by D. Martin).

1823)[7] described the lid as "thrown from its sarcophagus when it was forced open, and being reversed . . . remained buried by the stones, and unnoticed by any visitor."[8]

Although it is possible that the lid could have been toppled from the coffer after Bruce's departure, this would seem unlikely. Apart from the lack of any obvious reason for such vandalism, it seems unlikely that sufficient debris could then have entered the tomb to completely hide the lid by the 1810s (or even the 1790s: see below, page 131). The sarcophagus is also by no means as high as Bruce (even if exaggerating or rounding up) states. Accordingly, it seems far more likely that he is here describing a different tomb: that of Rameses IV (in KV2), which not only has a sarcophagus with a coffer-plus-lid height of approximately 300 centimeters (approximately 10 feet; that of Rameses III would have been only approximately 220 centimeters [about 7.2 feet] high), but also one with a lid that has remained in place since antiquity, with the side *of the coffer* broken away.[9]

There can be no doubt, however, about the identity of the tomb that is next described:

There have been some ornaments at the outer-pillars, or outer entry, which have been broken and thrown down. Thence you descend through an inclined passage, I suppose, about twenty feet broad; I speak only by guess, for I did not measure. The side-walls, as well as the roof of this passage, are covered with a coat of stucco, of a finer and more equal grain, or surface, than any I ever saw in Europe. I found my black-lead pencil little more worn by it than by writing upon paper.

Upon the left-hand side is the crocodile seizing upon the apis, and plunging him into the water. On the right-hand is the scarabus thebaicus, or the thebaic beetle, the first animal that is seen alive after the Nile retires from the land; and therefore thought to be an emblem of the resurrection. My own conjecture is, that the apis was the emblem of the arable land of Egypt; the crocodile, the typhon, or cacæodmon, the type of an over-abundant Nile; that the scarabaeus was the land which had been overflowed, and from which the water had soon retired, and has nothing to do with, the resurrection or immortality, neither of which at that time were in contemplation.

Farther forward on the right-hand of the entry, the pannels, or compartments, were still formed in stucco, but, in place of figures in relief, they were painted in fresco. I dare say this was the case on the left-hand of the passage, as well as the right. But the first discovery was so unexpected, and I had flattered myself that I should be so far master of my own time, as to see the whole at my leisure, that I was rivetted, as it were, to the spot by the first sight of these paintings, and I could proceed no further.

In one pannel were several musical instruments strowed upon the ground, chiefly of the hautboy kind, with a mouthpiece of reed. There were also some simple pipes or flutes. With them were several jars apparently of potter-ware which, having their mouths covered with parchment or skin, and being braced on their sides like a drum, were probably the instrument called the *tabor* or *tabret*; beat upon, by the hands, coupled in earliest ages with the harp, and preserved still in Abyssinia, though its companion, the last-mentioned instrument, is no longer known there.

In three following pannels were painted, in fresco, three harps, which merited the utmost attention, whether we consider the elegance of these instruments in their form, and the detail of their parts as they are here clearly expressed, or confine ourselves to the reflection that necessarily follows, to how great perfection music must have arrived, before an artist could have produced so complete an instrument as either of these.

As the first harp seemed to be the most perfect, and least spoiled, I immediately attached myself to this [fig. 123a], and desired my clerk [Luigi Balugani] to take upon him the charge of the second. In this way, by sketching exactly, and loosely, I hoped to have made myself master of all the paintings in that cave, perhaps to have extended my researches to others, though, in the sequel, I found myself miserably deceived . . . .

I look upon these harps then as the Theban harps in use in the time of Sesostris, who did not rebuild, but decorate ancient Thebes; I consider them as affording an incontestible proof, were they the only monuments remaining, that every art necessary to the construction, ornament, and use of this instrument, was in the highest perfection, and if so, all the others must have probably attained to the same degree.[10]

As a consequence of his enthusiastic descriptions of, and publication of his copies of, the harpers in the tomb, KV11 was long dubbed "Bruce's Tomb" or the "Harpers' Tomb."

However, in spite of Bruce's claim to have made, or have had made, careful copies of two of the harpers, William George Browne (1768–1813), who visited the tomb in 1792 (and left a graffito in either chamber Ja or Jb, indicating that he penetrated at least this far), was uncomplimentary in his account of the sepulcher:

a   b

FIGURE 123 a. The published version of Bruce's drawing of a harper in chamber Cd, with a modern photograph of the figure inset; b. Harpers in chamber Cd, as copied by the French expedition.

In the second part of the passage of the largest (tomb) are several cells or recesses on both sides. In these appear the chief paintings, representing the mysteries, which as well as the hieroglyphics covering all walls are very fresh. I particularly observed the two harpers described by Bruce; but his engraved figures seem to be from memory. The French merchants at [Cairo] informed me he brought with him two Italian artists; one was Luigi Balugani, a Bolognese, the other Zucci, a Florentine.[11]

Bonaparte in Egypt

These individual efforts were dwarfed by the activities of the scientific component of the French force that invaded Egypt under Napoleon Bonaparte in July 1798. As part of their survey, an elegant plan and section of the tomb of Rameses III was prepared,[12] although inaccuracies in the floor profile—in particular the complete omission of the descent within hall F, and a significant understatement of the depth of the crypt of the burial chamber—suggest that there was some quantity of debris in the rear part of the tomb when surveyed (cf. Pococke's failure to map this element six decades earlier); the sarcophagus coffer is shown lidless, with no sign of the cover. A number of tableaux and decorative elements from KV11 were included in the expedition's publication,[13] it being the principal tomb reproduced. However, the copies, some in color, concentrated on the annexes to corridor C, including, of course, the harpers (fig. 123b), with only a few isolated elements from other parts of the tomb.

Bonaparte's expedition also produced the first substantive documentation of the Medinet Habu memorial temple (called by them the "Palais"),[14] with plans, various views, and copies of selected tableaux; a number of decorative details were also presented, sometimes in color. These were not, however, published for some years, but Vivant Denon (1747–1825), part of the expedition, published a brief description in 1802.[15] The inner part of the temple was still largely filled with debris, but much of the outer walls were clear, resulting in a full copy of the Sea Peoples naval battle, and enlargements of some of the participants. Inside, the Festival of Min and (in color) the presentation of hands after the First Libyan War were shown in full in the final publication in the monumental *Description de l'Égypte*, while there was considerable coverage of the Eastern High Gate and its decoration. One thing noticeable about these copies is that in many cases hieroglyphs are omitted, presumably a result of both shortage of copying time and the continuing inability to read them. Another point of note is that they include restorations of damaged elements, rather than showing their current state. Rameses III's bark temple at Karnak was planned, and a few architectural and decorative elements drawn and published by the expedition.

Consuls and Collectors

Although the French were forced out of Egypt by the British in 1801, their activities, the consequent enhanced strategic importance of Egypt, and the advent of Muhammad Ali as Ottoman governor in 1805, with his drive to open up and modernize the country, led to a far greater awareness of, and interest in, its ancient culture. Many diplomats accredited to Muhammed Ali's court mixed their official work with the private collection of antiquities for (hopefully) sale, at a tidy profit, to their own (or other) governments. This was often through agents, the best known of whom was the aforementioned Giovanni Belzoni, who entered the employ of the recently arrived British consul-general, Henry Salt (1780–1827),[16] in 1816. Belzoni also undertook work on his own behalf, the dividing line between this work and that undertaken under the auspices of Salt being on occasion distinctly blurred.

From the autumn of 1816, Belzoni worked in the Valley of the Kings, opening, among others, the tombs of Ay (WV23), Montjuhirkopeshef C (son of Rameses IX, KV19), Rameses I (KV16) and, most famously, Sethy I (KV17).[17] He also undertook other work around the Valley and Western Thebes more generally, including the removal of the granite anthropoid coffin lid of the viceroy of Nubia Setau from his tomb, TT289 on the Dra Abu'l-Naga hill (fig. 48), in early 1817.[18] This had been "given" to him, while still in situ, by Salt's French opposite number, Bernardino Drovetti (1776–1852).[19]

Around the same time, Salt seems to have decided on the acquisition of the coffer of the sarcophagus of Rameses III: he certainly spent the winter of 1817–18 in the Valley,[20] including "superintend[ing] the making of a road from the tombs for the purpose of transporting a large sarcophagus"; but "one of the falls of water from the desert destroyed the whole road." However, in April 1818, he ceded its lid to Belzoni, described in the agreement as "the cover of a Sarcophagus found by him in one of the end-tombs of the Kings at Thebes."[21] It is unclear exactly when Belzoni removed this item, but it was certainly out of the tomb and with the rest of his principal finds on a boat that left Luxor for Rosetta and Alexandria on 27 January 1819.

The coffer was eventually removed from the tomb by Belzoni's successor in Salt's employ, Yanni D'Athanasi (1798–1854),[22] sometime between 1819 and 1824. He "caus[ed] all the colossal pieces which Belzoni had not taken away to be sent to Alexandria; above all, the famous sarcophagus of the tomb called Bruce's of which this celebrated traveler speaks so much."[23] D'Athanasi, no friend of Belzoni, alleges that the latter broke the lid into two pieces during the removal (although as the missing part does not seem to be in the tomb now, or emerged in any collection, it was more probably removed in antiquity).

The coffer went on to form part of the second of the three collections made by Salt. His first collection had been purchased by the British Museum in 1823, after considerable wrangling, for a price estimated by Salt as half his costs.[24] Although Salt was keen for the second to go to a British purchaser, or to the British government in exchange for a pension, he thus had no desire for further direct dealings with the British Museum as far as his second collection was concerned. Accordingly, it was consigned in 1825 to Leghorn in Italy for sale. There, it was viewed by Jean-François Champollion (1790–1832),[25] decipherer of hieroglyphs, who recommended purchase by France, which was finalized in February 1826.[26] The collection, including the sarcophagus coffer of Rameses III, thus went to the Louvre Museum in Paris.[27] It also included two bronze shabtis of the king (pages 117–18, above), presumably removed from the tomb at the same time. Salt may have given to Drovetti the bronze shabti of Rameses III that went to Turin in 1824.

The lid of the sarcophagus had initially been taken to the British Museum, as were other Belzoni items, including the calcite coffin of Sethy I. Although never displayed in Belzoni's 1821–22 exhibition at the Egyptian Hall on London's Piccadilly,[28] the lid was included in the catalogue for the sale of its exhibits in 1822, described as follows:

A cover from one of the kings' sarcophagi; this piece of antiquity was found in one of the kings' tombs in the Valley Beban el Malook, near its sarcophagus, from which it has been thrown to reach at the royal corpse; in the action of the depredation it has been partly mutilated at the lower end, but the upper part is quite perfect; it contains five, divinities, one in the centre is larger than life, in alto relief, the other four, in bas relief, represent the goddess Isis, and, perhaps, Buto, each holding a serpent with a woman's head, supposed to be the serpent Knuphis; all the faces and bodies are quite perfect to the lower part below the knees; the sarcophagus to which it belongs is still in the royal tomb in the above valley, and known by every traveller. The authenticity of its being the cover of one of the sarcophagi which contained the remains of one of the kings or Egypt, renders this piece most valuable, and worthy (of) the attention of the antiquarians. It is at present in the court-yard of the British Museum.[29]

The piece was not, however, sold, but was presented to the University of Cambridge's Fitzwilliam Museum through Belzoni's friend, the Rev. George Browne (1774–1843), who had helped raise money in Cambridge for Belzoni's final expedition, to West Africa, during which he died in Benin on 3 December 1823.[30] It would appear that the donation was in thanks for funds raised.

FIGURE 124 The lid of the sarcophagus of Rameses III on display in the Fitzwilliam Museum, Cambridge, around 1925. To the left is another early (1835) acquisition, the granite coffin of Hunefer (E.1.1835, reign of Rameses II), brought from Egypt by Barnard Hanbury in 1821.

The lid arrived in Cambridge on 31 March 1823 and was placed in the court of the Fitzwilliam Museum's building at the time, the former Perse School in Free School Lane (which now houses the Whipple Museum of the History of Science). By 1846, the lid, and other material, had been moved to the Pitt Press on Trumpington Street, but by 1856 it was in the present museum building, further down the same street, and which first opened in 1848. Published by Samuel Birch (1813–85), Keeper of Oriental Antiquities at the British Museum,[31] in 1879, in the late 1950s there were apparently discussions over reuniting the lid with the coffer in Paris, with the Fitzwilliam receiving a statue of Sekhmet from the Louvre in exchange,[32] but nothing came of this. Until 1968 the lid was displayed horizontally (fig. 124); it was then moved into its current vertical position.

Pictures and Words

Soon after the sarcophagus coffer had been removed, the tomb of Rameses III was visited by a number of Britons, including James Burton (1788–1862),[33] (Sir) John Gardner

Wilkinson (1797–1875),[34] Edward William Lane (1801–76),[35] and various members of the 1824–34 expedition led and funded by Robert Hay (1799–1873).[36] All made drawings of parts of the sepulcher (for example, figs. 125, 126), as well as drawings and descriptions of the king's temple at Medinet Habu, but only a small number have ever been published.[37]

A more comprehensive survey of the decoration of the tomb was made by the Franco-Tuscan expedition of 1828–29,[38] led by Champollion and Ippolito Rosellini (1800–43)[39] of Florence. This arrived in the Valley of the Kings early in 1829, and included some of the very first visitors to the tomb in modern times to have some understanding of the texts with which it, and other visible monuments of Rameses III, were adorned.

The placement of the king in history was rapidly identified by both scholars, as well as by Wilkinson, who characterized him as having (after a three-reign[40] gap following Rameses II)

FIGURE 125 Watercolor made of the burial chamber of KV11 by the Robert Hay expedition (BL Add MSS 29818 fol. 29).

FIGURE 126 The south wall of the burial chamber, as rendered by the Hay expedition (BL Add MSS 29820 fol. 123).

revived the taste for warlike operations, and the encouragement of the arts. Desirous
to rival the exploits of the second Rameses, he led an army into the east, stormed
the fortified places of the enemy; and either obliged them to take refuge in their
ships, or fitted out vessels of his own, to attack them. Perhaps indeed he may have
turned his arms against some other people, who lived near the sea coast, as their
dresses are different, and he is seen offering these prisoners to the god of Thebes in
a separate compartment, distinct from those he has taken in the land fight.

Returning victorious from the war he distributed rewards to his troops, and
employed himself in beautifying the cities of Egypt; with this view he constructed
a side temple, attached to the front court of Karnak, another at the sacred lake to
the south; and the temple of Medeenet Haboo, to which last he united his palace.
A change was also introduced into the mode of sculpturing the hieroglyphics, by
cutting the lower side to a great depth, while the upper inclined gradually from
the surface of the wall, till it reached the innermost part of the intaglio; so that the
hieroglyphics could be distinguished by a person standing immediately beneath,
and close to the wall, on which they were sculptured. This style was not imitated
by his successors, and the first change would seem to have been the first step
towards the decline and fall of the arts in Egypt; for though the sculptures of the
twenty-sixth dynasty evince a degree of detail, and increase of ornament, more
highly finished than those of the earlier periods, yet they fall far short in taste and
simplicity, in grandeur and design, of those executed from the reign of Osirtsen

I, to that of the third Rameses. Here too closes the most interesting period of Egyptian history. A long succession of princes many of whom bore the name of Rameses followed; but neither made themselves conspicuous by the construction of grand edifices at home, nor their exploits abroad.[41]

While Wilkinson gave Rameses the ordinal still employed today, Champollion and Rosellini were at that time calling him the fourth king of the name, having made two separate kings out of Rameses II,[42] based on the early 'short' and later 'long' versions of his prenomen, and an attempt to reconcile hieroglyphic sources with what later transpired to be the corrupt state of Manetho's extant data for the end of the Eighteenth and beginning of the Nineteenth Dynasties. As part of this, "Ramses IV" (that is, Rameses III) was put forward as the prototype of "Sethos-Ægyptus," the "Sethos, also called Ramessês" who appears in the writings of the first-century AD historian Titus Flavius Josephus (allegedly quoting Manetho) as a great conqueror. Nevertheless, Champollion and Rosellini correctly placed him, as had Wilkinson, subsequent to "Menephtah II" (Merenptah, "Menephtah I" being Sethy I), "Menephtah III" (Sethy II, with whom they linked Siptah and Tawosret), and "Uerri?" (the reading of Sethnakhte's prenomen at the time). On the other hand, their emerging chronology placed him three centuries too early as compared with modern views (accession in 1476 vs. 1173 on the chronology used in this book) and gave him an excessive reign of fifty-five years (based on Eusebius's data for "Sethôs"),[43] although it was noted that the king's highest extant monumental date known at the time was Year 16.[44] The king was also recognized as the husband of the woman now known as Iset D.

While much of the tomb of Rameses III was documented by the Franco-Tuscan expedition, full drawings were prepared and published[45] of only a few details, mainly from the already much-copied side chambers in corridors B and C. On the other hand, extensive notes were taken and published[46] of other parts of the tomb, including the innermost elements. That this was done is fortunate, since by the end of the century the innermost parts of the tomb had suffered significant flooding that destroyed, or at best ruined, much of their decoration, which thus only survives in these records, together with the drawings made by the Hay expedition (cf. figs. 107, 125, 126).[47]

Outside the Valley, the Franco-Tuscan team produced the first full copies of many reliefs at Rameses III's Medinet Habu memorial temple (dubbed by Champollion his "palais") and Eastern High Gate ("petit palais"). Most of the major narrative tableaux inside the first two courts and on the north exterior wall were drawn, thus making the war and Festival of Min reliefs available for wider study. The later addition of names to the processions of princes were also noted. Although no full copies were made of the decoration of the Karnak bark temple, notes were taken and eventually published.

The Medinet Habu complex was also extensively described by Wilkinson in his *Topography of Thebes*, published in 1835 as the first detailed 'guide' to the region,[48] while further documentation of the king's monuments was provided by the Prussian expedition of 1842–44.[49] This was under the leadership of Carl Richard Lepsius (1810–84),[50] who had now lowered Rameses's dates by some two centuries, compared with Rosellini, although they were still around a century too high, as compared with modern calculations.[51] Around the same time, Rameses III was also identified as the prototype for "Rhampsinitus," an Egyptian king who featured in a number of tales told by the fifth-century BC Greek writer Herodotus (Book II, 121–22),[52] and also potentially with another of the latter's legendary kings, Proteus (II, 113–14).[53] The desire to reconcile classical tradition with the Egyptian monuments died hard.

The year 1855 saw the discovery of one of the most fundamental sources for the study of the reign of Rameses III: the Great Harris Papyrus.[54] It was found along with other papyri in a hole in the rock in a robbed tomb somewhere between Medinet Habu and Deir el-Medina,[55] the group passing into the hands of the Alexandria-based British collector Anthony Harris (1790–1869),[56] who cut the roll into seventy-nine sections, pasting each onto cardboard. The document seems to have been first examined Egyptologically by August Adolf Eisenlohr (1832–1902),[57] of Heidelberg University, in 1869, who published his first assessments in 1872.[58]

The same year, Harris's entire collection was sold to the British Museum by his daughter Selima (ca. 1827–99),[59] a full publication being produced by Samuel Birch in 1876.[60] This included a long introduction providing an evaluation of the king's reign that served as the standard account for many years; Birch also published a popular translation in collaboration with Eisenlohr,[61] reflecting the importance given to the papyrus. The account of the reign produced by Birch was also able to factor in the data on the Harem Conspiracy from the Turin Judicial Papyrus, which had been first published by Théodule Devéria (1831–71) a few years previously,[62] and made available in English by Peter Le Page Renouf (1822–97) in 1876.[63]

Finding Pharaoh

All through this time, Rameses III's mummy lay hidden; however, it too would soon be revealed. The discovery of TT320 was made by three brothers of a local Qurnawi family, Muhammed (d. 1926), Ahmed (d. 1918/19), and Husein Abd el-Rassul,[64] either by accident or as part of a systematic search for tombs to rob (stories vary).[65] The date of their discovery is also unclear, perhaps in or before 1869, if a section of the papyrus of Queen Nedjmet A donated by King Edward VII to the British Museum in 1903 was acquired by him while in Egypt that year. The tomb was in any case certainly known before March 1874, when objects from it are definitely recorded as having been purchased by travelers. Key members of the Abd el-Rassul family were reported as saying that the discovery had been made in the summer of 1871.

The Abd el-Rassuls had been selling off material from the tomb—principally deriving from the burials of the Twenty-first Dynasty—for a number of years before suspicion fell upon them; Muhammad finally confessed on 25 June 1881 in exchange for an amnesty. On 5 July, Emile Brugsch (1842–1930),[66] keeper of Cairo's Bulaq Museum and at that time the most senior Antiquities Service official actually in the country (it was holiday season), arrived in Luxor with Ahmed Kamal (1851–1923),[67] its secretary–interpreter, and an inspector from Giza, Thadeos Matafian. Concerned for the security both of the tomb's contents and of himself, Kamal, and Matafian, Brugsch began clearance of the tomb on the morning of the seventh and it was completed the following day. The coffins and their contents arrived at Bulaq by boat from Luxor on the twenty-first.

A selection of coffins and mummies were immediately put on temporary display in the Central and Jewelry Galleries of the museum (fig. 127), pending the construction of a new, dedicated space, which was opened in October 1882; however, it was not until April 1886 that all the mummies and coffins were in glass cases. The mummy of Thutmose III was unwrapped by Brugsch in July 1881, but its badly damaged state discouraged further unwrappings for the time being. However, after two female mummies were unwrapped after showing signs of deterioration in 1883 and 1885, Gaston Maspero (1846–1916),[68] director of the Egyptian Antiquities Service, decided in 1886 that a number of the most important bodies should be unwrapped in a planned manner. This was begun on 1 June, when two bodies were dealt with in the presence of Khedive Tawfiq (r. 1879–92) himself.

One was that of Rameses II; the other mummy, found in a nameless cartonnage case (fig. 128a) within the colossal outer coffin of Queen Ahmes-Nefertiry,[69] was

> wrapped in an orange-red cloth, held by strips of ordinary cloth [fig. 128b]. It bore no inscription on the outside, but a headband of cloth covered with mystic figures was visible round the head, and intended to serve as amulets. As it was enclosed in the coffin of Neferetiry, for a long time it was thought to be the mummy of this queen. When it was opened . . . one saw, on the shroud of white cloth which came immediately under the envelope of orange cloth, a hieratic inscription of four lines (fig. 115).[70]

This recorded the 'Osirification' of Rameses III in Year 13 of Nesibanebdjedet I (see pages 120–21, above).

FIGURE 127 The selection of royal and high-priestly coffins and mummies as provisionally displayed in the Bulaq Museum at the end of July 1881. In the rear corners of the room are the coffin lid and mummy board of Panedjem I (CG61024–5), with the rear row of coffins comprising (from the left) those of Nesikhonsu (CG61030), Masaharta (CG61027), Maatkare (CG61028), Tayuheret (CG61032), and Nedjmet A (CG61024). In the front row can be seen the coffin of Siamun A (CG61008), the lid and trough/mummy of Amenhotep I (CG61005/61058), the coffin/mummy of Rameses III (CG61021/61083), and the coffin of Thutmose II (CG61013). Rameses III's grouping with individuals of the early Eighteenth Dynasty is owing to the belief at this time that the mummy was that of Ahmes-Nefertiry, mother of Amenhotep I.

A black ink drawing accompanied this inscription: a ram-headed hawk that holds two flabella in its claws [fig. 128c]. His wings fold over his head, as if to form a necklace for the mummy. The name "Amun," traced in ink, to the left of the head, allowed us to understand that this was an image of Amun . . . . Three thicknesses of bandages, without inscription, succeeded this first shroud, then we were stopped by a sewn and stitched canvas shroud. This being opened with scissors, new layers of cloth could be seen through the opening. Some of them bore inscriptions or images in black ink. One reads on one of them [the name and titles of the high priest Panedjem I] and, on another, the same formula, with

FIGURE 128 a. The coffin used for Rameses III's reburial (Cairo CG61021); b. the mummy as found; c. the latter with its outer wrappings removed; d. the mummy (Cairo CG61083) at the end of the unwrapping process, still largely encased in its resin-soaked carapace.

the date of the Year 10 . . . . A piece of cloth depicts the god Amun . . . with a human head sitting on his throne; a line of cursive hieroglyphs below tells us that this cloth was made by . . . the Chantress of Amun, Faienmut, daughter of the high priest of Amun, Piankh . . . . [A] fragment found in the coffin of Neferetiry is of the same type as that of Piankh's daughter. [On another] King Rameses III, standing in front of an altar, the Blue Crown on the head, offers the wine to two human-headed [forms of god Amun]. This bandage was made by the chief washerman of the king . . . , the characters half in hieroglyphs, half in hieratic. So many different testimonies would have sufficed to establish the identity of the marriage: by continuing the operation, a more decisive proof was found. Two pectorals were hidden under the folds of the fabric, the first, in gilded wood [fig. 129, right], had only the ordinary representation of Isis and Nephthys adoring the sun, but the other was pure gold, and showed on the two faces Ramses III in adoration before the two forms of Amun mentioned above on the strip of the chief washerman [fig. 129, left]. A final canvas sheath, [and then] a last shroud of red cloth; the body was in good condition, but the face was embedded in a compact mass of tar. This covering was removed with a chisel by M. Barsanti[71] [fig. 128d], measurements being taken, on the 6th of June, by MM. Fouquet,[72] Bouriant,[73] Insinger,[74] and by me. [The] height from the top of the head to the soles of the feet was 1m 683[mm].

The hair and beard are shaved. The nose, like that of Rameses II, was slightly depressed by the bandages. The mouth is thin: only five teeth are visible; the first molar was used or cased. The ears are round; the lobe is not very developed and the edge very strong. The lobe had been pierced, but any earrings had been removed in antiquity. The genitals have been cut to be embalmed apart.[75]

As only the head of the mummy was thus exposed, various comments down to 2012, suggesting that a lack of wounds on the body argued against the king having actually been murdered as a result of the Harem Conspiracy,[76] were without basis, since no examination of anything below the neck was possible!

FIGURE 129 The two pectorals found on the mummy of Rameses III. The left-hand example was made of two plates of gold, fitted back to back, the other of wood, gilded on the front (Cairo CG52005-6).

When the anatomist Elliot Smith (1871–1937)[77] undertook his re-examination of the royal mummies during the first decade of the twentieth century, he could do little more than quote the above observations on Rameses III's mummy, owing to the continued presence of the carapace. He did, however, suggest that X-rays could be useful in clearing up a number of issues, although as it turned out it would be half a century before this could be done.[78]

Once partially unwrapped, the mummy conformed to the peregrinations of the other royal mummies, moving in 1889, together with the rest of the museum collection, to a former palace in Giza which opened on 12 January 1890.[79] This was only regarded as a temporary location for the institution, pending the 1902 completion of a purpose-built museum on what is today Midan Tahrir in Cairo. There, the royal mummies were placed in the western gallery at the rear of the upper floor of the new building (as of 2018 designated Gallery 7, and for many years holding part of the Tutankhamun collection).

In 1928, a general decision was taken to no longer display unwrapped mummies, and thus such bodies were either placed back in their coffins, which remained on display with their lids closed, or moved to a special room, access to which required ministerial permission. From 1931 to 1936, the principal royal mummies were housed in the pharaonic-style mausoleum commissioned to hold the body of the politician Saad Zaghlul (1859–1927), founder of the Wafd party, but then appropriated by a new anti-Wafd government to be a national pantheon.[80] With a return to power by the Wafd in May 1936, however, this decision was reversed, Zaghlul's body being reburied in the mausoleum, and the pharaohs evacuated to storerooms back at the museum.

Water and Ruin

While the mummy of Rameses III had come to light in 1881, his surviving original coffin trough remained lost until 1898, when the tomb of Amenhotep II was found by Victor Loret (1859–1946).[81] As for Rameses III's own tomb in the Valley, although Eugéne Lefébure (1838–1908)[82] had been able to make notes and sketches of the decoration of KV11 in the early 1880s as part of his extensive survey of its tombs,[83] by the end of the century the condition of the inner parts was rapidly deteriorating, owing to the penetration of water and water-borne material.

None of this water had entered, however, via the entrance to the tomb, as had been the case with most instances of flooding in the Valley of the Kings.[84] One source of flooding in KV11 was the breakthrough from KV10, a tomb which had already received significant water-deposited material by the 1820s, and still more by the early 1880s.[85] Another source was cracks in the rock, leading from the surface directly into the innermost rooms of the tomb. These only seem to have begun channeling water into the sepulcher late in the nineteenth century, resulting in water on occasion standing up to four meters deep in burial chamber J. Such inundations are known to have occurred in 1890 and 1910; between these episodes, in 1895, some clearance work was carried out by the Egyptian Antiquities Service, but although the outer parts of the tomb, up to and including chamber F, were made accessible to tourists, access beyond corridor G was barred by a gate, the inner rooms being regarded as now irretrievably ruinous.

Princes and Queens

The tombs of Queens Iset (QV51) and Tyti (QV52) had, like that of the king himself, seemingly stood open since antiquity, both being recorded by the Franco-Tuscan, Hay, and Prussian expeditions, and likewise those of Princes Prehirwenemef (QV42) and Rameses (QV53). That of Tyti caused early confusion, the queen being variously confused with Tiye A, wife of Amenhotep III,[86] and Tey, wife of Ay;[87] it was not until Lepsius suggested that the lady of QV52 might actually be a Twentieth Dynasty queen[88] that views began to change. Georges Bénédite (1857–1926)[89] published Tyti's sepulcher in 1894, including color renditions of the reliefs (for example, fig. 130), but it was not until 1903, when the Italian Mission under Ernesto Schiaparelli (1856–1928)[90] began work, that new tombs were opened in the Valley of the Queens, and already known ones systematically cleared and recorded.[91] Among new discoveries were the sepulchers of Sethhirkopeshef C (QV43), Khaemwaset E (QV44—found containing many late-Third Intermediate Period intrusive burials), and Amenhirkopeshef B (QV55).

In the wake of the Italian discoveries, Scottish Egyptologist Colin Campbell (1848–1931)[92] produced a popular treatment of the most spectacular of the 'new' tombs (that of Rameses II's wife Nefertiry [QV66]), together with the 'old' sepulcher of Tyti.[93] In dealing with the latter, Campbell discussed the question of the identity of the queen, sadly accepting that "the royal lady for whom it was executed has (now) fallen from the eminence and splendour of being the consort of one of the most illustrious of Egyptian potentates, Amenhotep III, . . . down to the comparative obscurity of the wife of an insignificant Rameses of the XXth Dynasty." As already noted (page 62), it would not be for another century that the question of Tyti's exact place in history was finally resolved.

Epigraphy Triumphant

Although many details of the Medinet Habu temple had been copied by the Napoleonic and various nineteenth-century expeditions, work had focused on a relatively limited number of tableaux, especially the 'historical' reliefs. Given restrictions on time and resources, this was perfectly understandable, and such 'cherry picking' was standard practice at the time. It was not until the inauguration of the Archaeological Survey

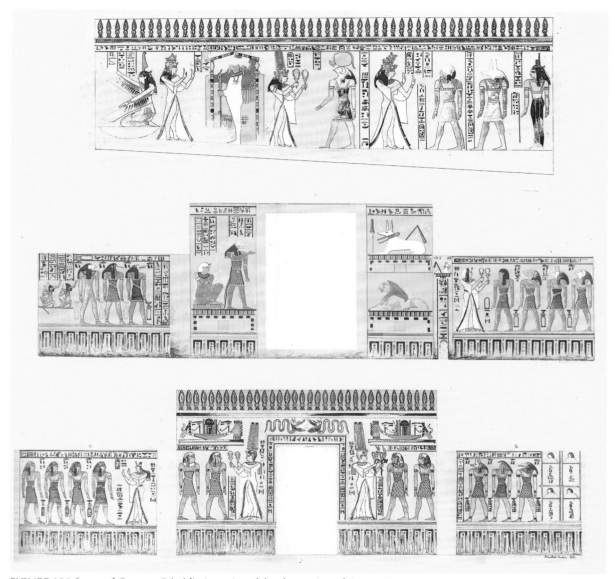

FIGURE 130 Some of Georges Bénédite's copies of the decoration of Queen Tyti's QV52.

of Egypt by the British Egypt Exploration Fund in 1890, with its purpose to produce comprehensive facsimile copies of all standing monuments at a given site, that the idea of comprehensive copying and publication of a given monument or group of monuments began to become an accepted goal.[94]

This concept was picked up by the American Egyptologist James Henry Breasted (1865–1935),[95] who in 1906 had included an exhaustive set of translations of texts relating to Rameses III in his monumental *Ancient Records of Egypt*, while also noting that the Medinet Habu temple was "still as a whole practically unpublished."[96] Much still remained to be excavated as well, although, in early 1913, Harry Burton (1879–1940),[97] working for the businessman Theodore Davis (1838–1915), almost at the very end of the latter's excavating career in Egypt,[98] had cleared some of the palace.[99]

In 1924, Breasted established the University of Chicago's Epigraphic Survey at Luxor under Harold Nelson (1878–1954),[100] with funding from the oil magnate John D. Rockefeller, Jr. (1874–1960),[101] with the excavation and full documentation of Medinet Habu as its first objective.[102] The aim was to produce the most precise facsimiles possible, printed on a generous scale to maximize the levels of detail in the drawings and supplementary photographs.

Based first at the 'old' Chicago House on the west bank (a new complex on the east bank replaced it in 1931; the original building now houses the Marsam Hotel), work began on copying the reliefs on the north exterior wall of the memorial temple in November 1924. In 1926, excavation work was added to the program under Uvo Hölscher (1878–1963),[103] who had published a study of the Eastern High Gate in 1910. He and Nelson published the first of a series of joint preliminary reports in 1929. The following year, the first full publication appeared, providing background to the whole project, an overview of the entire Medinet Habu complex, and, as its fundamental purpose, facsimile drawings of the tableaux on the north exterior wall west of the First Pylon, together with the related reliefs on that pylon and on the south side of the Second Court. The rest of the 'historical' depictions were published in 1932 (translations following in 1936),[104] with volumes covering the remainder of the main temple coming out in 1934, 1940, 1957, 1963, and 1964. The last part, dealing with the Eastern High Gate, was published in 1970, making the whole of the decoration of Rameses's greatest monument finally available to scholarship.[105]

Hölscher's parallel excavations not only exposed those parts of the monument that still remained partly encumbered (including the palace), but also permitted a detailed architectural and archaeological study of the whole structure. The publication of his work was issued in two parts, in 1941 and 1951. A guidebook to the temple and its surrounding monuments, based on the Chicago work, appeared from the pen of the Chicago House deputy director, William Murnane (1943–2000),[106] in 1980.

In addition to the work at Medinet Habu, copying was also undertaken at the long-neglected temples of Rameses III at Karnak. The bark temple had been cleared by Georges Legrain (1865–1917)[107] during 1896/7, with considerable subsequent conservation and repair, and that in the Mut precinct by Maurice Pillet (1881–1964)[108] in 1922. The two temples' publication by the Chicago team appeared in two parts, in 1936.

A consolidated hand-copy digest of historical and biographical texts from all sources from the reign of Rameses III was published by Kenneth Kitchen (b. 1932), of the University of Liverpool, in 1983, with translations following in 2008,[109] and additional material added in 1989/2014[110] and 2018.[111] These additions particularly reflected the ongoing publication of the material from Deir el-Medina. A volume of notes and comments to the texts and their translations is in preparation by Kitchen's student, Benedict Davies.

Under the Wrappings

The royal mummies were returned to display in 1945, in Gallery 52 in the southwest corner of the museum. Two decades later, in 1967, they were here the subject of X-ray examination by a mission from the Universities of Michigan and Alexandria, thus finally allowing a glimpse within Rameses III's bodily covering.[112] Little was revealed, save indications of arteriosclerosis, the presence of three amulets from the Four Sons of Horus within the thoracic cage, and that, unlike almost all the royal mummies, it was free from post-mortem damage caused by robbers or careless embalmers.

The king's dental health was assessed as showing "Moderate" attrition, with "Fair" periodontal health.[113] His age at death was assessed as "30:0–35:0" years[114]—which was, of course, completely inconsistent with a man who reigned for thirty-two years, and was militarily active from at least his Year 5. While there have been tentative attempts to cast doubt on the identity of the mummy,[115] the presence of not only dockets naming him but also two pectorals in his name on the mummy make it very difficult to question its attribution.

The problem of 'under-aging' is not, however, unique to this mummy: a considerable number of other kings were given wholly unlikely ages at death as a result of the Michigan/Alexandria work.[116] That the problem of aging non-recent human remains concerns not just those of ancient Egyptians has been made clear by studies carried out on over a thousand sets of eighteenth- to nineteenth-century AD human remains recovered from the crypts of Christ Church, Spitalfields, in London.[117] Of these, nearly half were of individuals whose age at death was indicated by coffin plates but, when assessed against the conventional anatomical criteria used in archaeology for aging skeletal remains, less than 30 percent of the sample was correctly placed within five years of the real age, and only 50 percent within ten years. Among cases of under-aging, individuals who were known certainly to have died in their late eighties, or their nineties, appeared according to the anatomical criteria to be in their sixties, or in one case late fifties! Thus, all determinations of age reached by applying current forensic criteria to premodern (or even early modern) humans carry very significant margins of error, particularly once the individual being studied has reached adulthood.

The mummies remained on show until 1981, when President Anwar Sadat (1918–81) ordered that the gallery be closed. It was not until 1994 that the Eighteenth and Nineteenth Dynasty kings were conserved and partly rewrapped—with their faces left exposed—before being moved to new high-specification cases in gallery 56 at the opposite end of the south range of the museum. Gallery 52 was later refurbished to contain the later royal and high-priestly mummies, including Rameses III. The king remained in Tahrir Square until 15 June 2019, when he and twenty-four other royal or high-priestly mummies were moved to purpose-designed galleries in the new National Museum of Egyptian Civilization (NMEC) at Fustat, in southern Cairo.

During the 2010s, a number of mummies, including that of Rameses III, were examined using computed tomography.[118] On the basis of this new imaging, the king's age was pushed up to "about 60" years and the previously seen Four Sons of Horus amulets fully defined—as were his allegedly "missing" genitals (page 142, above). Most dramatically, however, the scans identified "a cut wound in the soft tissues of the lower neck that extends from the lower end of the fifth to the seventh cervical vertebrae, causing a gap in the soft tissues of the neck that measures 35 mm and extends deeply to reach the bone. All the structures of the neck (trachea, esophagus, and large blood vessels) were severed. The extent and depth of the wound would indicate that the injury was fatal."[119] A *wadjet*-eye amulet had been placed in the wound, perhaps to magically 'heal' it. An additional injury inflicted around the time of death, identified by the same study, was the partial amputation of the left big toe by a sharp blade, with at least four more *wadjet*-eye amulets placed within the wrappings of the feet.[120]

Having thus finally proved that Rameses III had died by violence, the same team investigated the long-mooted idea that a mysterious mummy, "Unknown Man E," found in the TT320 cache, and showing various anomalous features,[121] might be his rebel son Pentaweret. The mummy was assessed as belonging to a person eighteen to twenty years of age, and while it has been unable to prove cause of death, suggestions were made that a compressed fold of skin around the neck might indicate suffocation by strangulation or hanging. A DNA analysis showed that the mummy and that of Rameses III shared a Y-chromosome haplotype (DNA sequence), suggesting that they were related. However, the published conclusion that this actually demonstrated a father–son relationship, and that Unknown Man E should be regarded as Pentaweret, seems to overstate what the present evidence can show, especially, as the researchers admitted, in the absence of any genetic data on Pentaweret's mother.[122] Thus the question of the mummy's relationship to Rameses III must remain open for the time being.

Publishing the Tomb

Although its innermost parts were in a poor state, the tomb of Rameses III continued to be an important monument in the history of Egyptian royal tombs, as the last one in the Valley of the Kings to be completely finished, both decoratively and structurally. During the 1930s, a concession to copy the tomb was granted to the Chicago Oriental Institute, with the work to be carried out by Alfred-Wilhelm Bollacher (1877–1968), an artist who had previously worked on blocks from the pyramid of Sahure at Abusir before the First World War. However, only a small part of the decoration of chamber Bb was ever copied.[123]

Then, during the late 1950s, Tadeusz Andrzejewski (1923–61) began work on publishing the tomb,[124] and had apparently nearly completed his fieldwork at the time of his untimely death.[125] However, only one article, on the Book of Gates in the burial chamber, ever appeared, posthumously in 1962, although some of his material from KV11 appeared in the studies of the *Amduat* and Litany of Re produced by Erik Hornung (b. 1933) soon afterward.[126] Another Polish scholar, Marek Marciniak (1937–96), began work in the tomb in 1977, but although his fieldwork was completed in 1979, only a preliminary report and a discussion of a constructional aspect of the tomb had appeared before his likewise untimely death.[127]

A further project to publish the tomb, and also make the inner rooms once more accessible, was begun by the Ramesses III (KV 11) Publication and Conservation Project, led by Anke Weber, in 2009. This intends to record the tomb using modern methods and fully integrate this with all extant published and archival sources. By 2014, chambers Ba–Ch, Fa, and J had been recorded, with Jc completed in 2016, and a preliminary report published.[128]

Rameses III: Paper Tiger?

In spite of the extensive depictions of military activities on Rameses III's monuments, and the description of some of them in pHarris I, doubts concerning their reality began to emerge in the early twentieth century.[129] Among the first doubters was Henry Hall (1873–1930), Keeper of Egyptian and Assyrian Antiquities at the British Museum,[130] who opined in 1927 that the Euphrates-area place names mentioned by Rameses III had been copied from Thutmose III, and were thus of little use in determining the extent of Rameses's activities in the north, and that both the Sea Peoples and Syrian campaigns were actually of strictly limited scope.

In later decades, this skepticism was deepened to an idea that Rameses III's battle tableaux were not only largely copied from those of Rameses II, but that those depicting

FIGURE 131 The Eastern High Gate between 1890 and 1910.

Nubians and Syrians might be to a greater or lesser extent fictional as far as the third Rameses was concerned.[131] This was taken a further step forward in 1980 when Leonard Lesko (b. 1938), then at the University of California, Berkeley, argued that *all* Rameses III's war reliefs at Medinet Habu, save those depicting the Year 11 Libyan campaign, were probably nothing more than copies of now-lost tableaux in the memorial temple of Merenptah, used in a 'generic' manner and providing no evidence for Rameses III's own activities.[132] Even the pHarris I narrative, hitherto felt to be more 'factual,' was suggested to have been produced on the basis of the Medinet Habu reliefs, and thus also not to be trusted. While few have accepted this ultra-minimalist approach in toto, the idea that Rameses III overstated his military activities was well embedded in the generally accepted historical picture by the end of the twentieth century. Kenneth Kitchen openly doubted that the Year 12 Syrian campaign ever took place,[133] while Karl Strobel (b. 1954), of Alpen-Adria-Universität Klagenfurt, was prepared to allow Rameses III a Year 5 Libyan campaign—but nothing else—as late as 2011.[134]

However, during the twenty-first century, the originality, and hence likely veracity, of many of the war tableaux was beginning to be recognized. Although the Sea Peoples campaign had generally been accepted as 'real' by everyone other than the 'ultra-minimalists,' the divergences between the presentations of Merenptah and Rameses III—and thus the unlikelihood of copying—now became much clearer.[135] Likewise, Dan'el Kahn (b. 1969), of the University of Haifa, demonstrated that Rameses III's Nubian campaign reliefs were *not* mechanical copies of those of Rameses II,[136] and also that none of Rameses III's Asiatic tableaux corresponded to any potential source depictions on Rameses II's monuments.[137]

Indeed, the former skeptic Kitchen began to take a more positive view of the idea that Rameses III *did* operate in northern Syria, albeit still doubtful that the king's topographical lists contained more than a kernel of contemporary reality;[138] however, others were now highlighting the uniqueness of significant parts of them as well.[139] Kitchen also now took to task a deconstruction of the Sea Peoples texts that had in 1991 attempted to deny that a substantive military event had happened in Year 8.[140] The idea that Rameses III's reach was far greater than some had hitherto thought was further bolstered by the discovery in 2011 of the inscription of the king at Tayma, deep in the Arabian desert (page 48, above). Thus, although doubts still remain in some areas, the scale and area of the military activities claimed by Rameses III now seem less open to doubt than was the case during the latter part of the twentieth century, resulting in a revived appreciation of him as indeed "the last great pharaoh."[141]

Chronology

LE = Lower Egypt only; UE = Upper Egypt.
All New Kingdom and Third Intermediate Period dates are based on the scheme set
out in Dodson 2019a; in any case, all are more or less conjectural prior to 690 BC.
Parentheses indicate a co-ruler.

EARLY DYNASTIC PERIOD

Dynasty 1	3050–2810 BC
Dynasty 2	2810–2660

OLD KINGDOM

Dynasty 3	2660–2600
Dynasty 4	2600–2470
Dynasty 5	2470–2360
Dynasty 6	2360–2195

FIRST INTERMEDIATE PERIOD

Dynasties 7/8	2195–2160
Dynasties 9/10 (LE)	2160–2040
Dynasty 11a (UE)	2160–2065

MIDDLE KINGDOM

Dynasty 11b	2065–1994
Dynasty 12	1994–1780
Dynasty 13	1780–1650

SECOND INTERMEDIATE PERIOD

Dynasty 14 (LE)	1700–1650
Dynasty 15 (LE)	1650–1535
Dynasty 16 (UE)	1650–1590
Dynasty 17 (UE)	1585–1540
Ahmose the Elder	
Taa	
Kamose	–1540

NEW KINGDOM

Dynasty 18	
Ahmose I	1540–1516
Amenhotep I	1516–1496
Thutmose I	1496–1481
Thutmose II	1481–1468
Thutmose III	1468–1415
(Hatshepsut	1462–1447)
Amenhotep II	1415–1386
Thutmose IV	1386–1377
Amenhotep III	1377–1337
Akhenaten	1337–1321
(Smenkhkare	1325–1323)
(Neferneferuaten	1322–1319)
Tutankhamun	1321–1312
Ay	1312–1308
Horemheb	1308–1278
Dynasty 19	
Rameses I	1278–1276
Sethy I	1276–1265
Rameses II	1265–1200
Merenptah	1200–1190
Sethy II	1190–1185
(Amenmeses [UE]	1189–1186)
Siptah	1186–1178
Tawosret	1178–1176
Dynasty 20	
Sethnakhte	1176–1173
Rameses III	1173–1142
Rameses IV	1142–1136

Rameses V	1136–1132
Rameses VI	1132–1125
Rameses VII	1125–1118
Rameses VIII	1118–1116
Rameses IX	1116–1098
Rameses X (UE)	1098–1095
Rameses XI	1110–1095 (LE) + 1095–1078

THIRD INTERMEDIATE PERIOD

Dynasty 21	
Herihor (UE)	1078–1065
Nesibanebjedet I (LE)	1078–1053
Amenemnesut (UE?)	1065–1049
Panedjem I (UE)	1063–1041
Pasebkhanut I	1049–999
Amenemopet	1001–992
Osorkon the Elder	992–985
Siamun	985–867
Pasebkhanut II	967–941
Dynasty 22	943–736
Dynasty 23	736–666
Dynasty 24	734–721
Dynasty 25	754–656

SAITE PERIOD

Dynasty 26	664–525

LATE PERIOD

Dynasty 27	525–404
Dynasty 28	404–399
Dynasty 29	399–380
Dynasty 30	380–342
Dynasty 31	342–332

HELLENISTIC PERIOD

Dynasty of Macedonia	332–310
Dynasty of Ptolemy	310–30

ROMAN PERIOD

30 BC–AD 395

NOTES

Notes to Introduction

1   Epigraphic Survey 1930–70; Hölscher 1941–51.
2   Grandet 1993.
3   Cline and O'Connor 2012b.

Notes to Chapter 1

1   See page 148, below, for an estimate of his age at death as "about 60"; counting back, the cumulative total of Rameses III's own thirty-two years of reign, Sethnakhte's two of sole rule, Siptah and Tawosret's eight, Sethy II's six (embracing Amenmeses's whole reign) and Merenptah's ten is fifty-eight years.
2   For the convention of distinguishing homonyms by letters and upper- and lower-case Roman numerals, see Dodson and Hilton 2010: 39.
3   Cf. Dodson 2019b: 9–10.
4   For which see Dodson 2016a.
5   On Senenmut's sarcophagus and its close similarities to contemporary royal ones, in particular that of Hatshepsut, see Hayes 1950.
6   Kitchen 1968–90: V, 671–72[251]; 1993–2014: V, 7–8[251(13)].
7   pBM EA9999, §75,4–5 (Erichsen 1933: 91; Grandet 1994: pl. 76).
8   See Dodson 2018: 63–65, 117–19.
9   oPetrie UC19614 (Kitchen 1968–90: V, 1–2).
10 Kitchen 1993–2014: VII, 179–82; Roberson 2018: 71–72[199].
11 Cf. Hornung 2006: 214 on the apparent ten-year gap between Year 7 of Tawosret and Year 7 of Rameses III.
12 von Beckerath 1994: 77 n.431.
13 Stockholm E.1393 (Kitchen 1968–90: V, 2[3]; 1993–2014: V, 2[3]).
14 Kitchen 1968–90: V, 1[1]; 1993–2014: V, 1[1].
15 Kitchen 1968–90: V, 3[4]; 1993–2014: V, 2–3[4].
16 Kitchen 1968–90: V, 3–4[5]; 1993–2014: V, 3–4[5].
17 Porter and Moss 1960–64: 518–26; Thomas 1966: 125–27; Reeves 1990: 115; Marciniak 1982; 1983; Weeks 2000: 19; Weeks 2001: 232–39; Weber 2018.
18 Porter and Moss 1972: 447; R.H. Wilkinson 2011; Creasman, Johnson, McClain, and Wilkinson 2014; cf. McClain and Johnson 2013.

Notes to Chapter 2

1   For a fuller compendium, see von Beckerath 1999: 164–67.

2   On Khaemwaset C, see Fisher 2001: I, 89–105; II, 89–143.

3   Kitchen 1968–90: V, 258–59[80–82]; 1993–2014: V, 216–17[80–82].

4   Kitchen 1968–90: V, 259–68[83–86]; 1993–2014: V, 217–23[83–86].

5   Kitchen 1968–90: V, 268–69[87]; 1993–2014: V, 223–24[87].

6   Malinine, Posener, and Vercoutter 1968: 15–16.

7   Kitchen 1968–90: V, 270[89]; 1993–2014: V, 225[89].

8   Kitchen 1968–90: V, 270–71[90, 91, 93]; 1993–2014: V, 225–26[90, 91, 93]; on Rameses III's Middle Egyptian activities, see also Christophe 1953.

9   Kemp 1995: 447–48.

10   Kitchen 1968–90: V, 271[92]; 1993–2014: V, 226[92].

11   Kitchen 1968–90: V, 272[94]; 1993–2014: V, 227[94].

12   Bunbury, Graham, and Hunter 2008.

13   Porter and Moss 1972: 27–34.

14   Porter and Moss 1972: 228–44.

15   Such dismantling is, however, unlikely to have begun until after Year 29 of Rameses III, as the temple was still functioning in this year (see ch. 2 n. 91, below).

16   McClain et al. 2011.

17   Breasted 1906: 116 note c.

18   Porter and Moss 1972: 273–74.

19   Kitchen 1968–90: V, 338[133]; 1993–2014: V, 287–88[133].

20   Kitchen 1968–90: V, 340–41[135]; 1993–2014: V, 289–90[135].

21   Kitchen 1968–90: V, 339[134]; 1993–2014: V, 288–89[134].

22   Kitchen 1968–90: V, 341–42[136]; 1993–2014: V, 290–91[136].

23   Kitchen 1968–90: V, 346[139]; 1993–2014: V, 293–94[139].

24   Kitchen 1968–90: VI, 880[119]; 1993–2014: VI, 599[119].

25   Kitchen 1968–90: VI, 461[12]; 1993–2014: VI, 355–56[12].

26   See discussion in D.B. Redford 2018: 142–51.

27   As evidenced by contemporary diplomatic correspondence, in particular the Amarna Letters (for which see Moran 1992).

28   Manassa 2003.

29   This and other proposed equations of 'Sea Peoples' names with later entities go back to the mid-nineteenth century, in particular de Rougé 1867 and Chabas 1872: 299–328, although the identification of the Peleset goes back to at least 1846 (see Vandersleyen 1985: 39–41).

30   For an overview, see Cline and O'Connor 2003; 2012a.

31   pBM EA9999, §76,6–77,6 (Erichsen 1933: 92–94; Grandet 1994: I, 336–37).

32   For recent overviews and discussions of the Medinet Habu war tableaux, see Ben-Dor Evian 2016; D.B. Redford 2018.

33   D.B. Redford 2018: 1–20.

34   Kitchen 1968–90: V, 22–23[4]; 1993–2014: V, 20–21[4].

35   Both suggestions go back to Brugsch 1879: 854–56, 820–23.

36   D.B. Redford 2018: 21–41.

37   Kitchen 1968–90: V, 40[9]; 1993–2014: V, 34[9].

38   For a recent discussion, see D.B. Redford 2018: 111–28.

39   On the location of the battles of the campaign, cf. D.B. Redford 2018: 130–32.

40   Cf. D.B. Redford 2018: 153–59.

41   Ben-Dor Evian 2017.

42   A letter to the local king, Ammurapi, has been dated on the basis of its having been written by the Egyptian chancellor Bay

(Freu 1988), but the titles given to the sender in the letter are wholly at variance with those known for him from Bay's undoubted monuments, making it all but certain that we are dealing with a different person, in spite of widespread non-Egyptological approval (e.g., Cline 2014: 109).

43 For references, see Cline 2014: 192 n.29.

44 Kaniewski et al. 2011.

45 References in Cline 2014: 192 n.30.

46 Weinstein 1992: 143, with references.

47 See Cline 2014: 114–21.

48 Cline 2014: 124–26.

49 Mountjoy 1999; 2006.

50 Cline 2014: 128–32, with references.

51 Cline 2014: 132–35, with references.

52 Cf. Cline 2014: 137–70, with references. The events are likely to have found echoes in later literature, with many suggesting that Homer's Trojan War narrative has roots in conflicts of this time; see D.B. Redford 2018: 128–29, for suggestions as to links with the legendary figure of Mopsos.

53 Kitchen 1968–90: V, 58–66[16]; 1993–2014: V, 47–52 [16].

54 Kitchen 1968–90: V, 57–58[15]; 1993–2014: V, 46–47[15].

55 Kitchen 1968–90: V, 48–54[11], 56[14]; 1993–2014: V, 40–44[11], 46[14].

56 Kitchen 1968–90: V, 43–48[10]; 1993–2014: V, 36–39[10].

57 Kitchen 1968–90: V, 54–56[12–13]; 1993–2014: V, 44–45[12–13].

58 Kitchen 1968–90: V, 67–71[17]; 1993–2014: V, 52–55[17]; D.B. Redford 2018: 42–69.

59 Leahy 1990; Snape 2003.

60 Kitchen 1968–90: V, 78–88[21–24]; 1993–2014: V, 60–67[21–24]; D.B. Redford 2018: 134–51.

61 Kitchen 1968–90: V, 92–100[27–28]; 1993–2014: V, 71–77[27–28].

62 Kitchen 1968–90: II, 260[68ivβ]; V, 109[36c], 110[37c], 111[38]; 1993–2014: II: 101[68ivb]; V, 85[36c], 86–87[37c], 87[38].

63 See Kahn 2011; James 2017; D.B. Redford 2018: 143–47.

64 Bryce 1998: 381–91.

65 Kitchen 1968–90: II, 268–81[68]; 1993–2014: II: 99–110[68].

66 Porter and Moss 1952: 378–79, 380, 391; Higginbotham 1999.

67 Cf. Gaballa 1976.

68 Although less dark than was once thought (see Dickinson 2006).

69 Kitchen 1968–90: V, 72–77[19–20]; 1993–2014: V, 55–60[19–20].

70 Kitchen 1968–90: V, 8–9[1]; 1993–2014: V, 9–10[1]; D.B. Redford 2018: 1.

71 See chapter 2, note 95, below.

72 Breasted 1906: 202–204; Grandet 1994: I, 338–39.

73 Meeks 2003.

74 Cf. Bongrani 1997.

75 For a brief discussion, see James 2017: 77 n.73.

76 Kitchen 1968–90: V, 257[78C–D]; 1993–2014: V, 216[78C–D].

77 Kitchen 1968–90: V, 248[73]; 1993–2014: V, 210[73].

78 Somaglino and Tallet 2011; 2013.

79 For the ḥb-sd, see Hornung and Staehelin 1974.

80 pTurin C1880 (Gardiner 1948: pl. 55, l.15–16).

81 Gardiner 1910.

82 Kitchen 1968–90: IV, 281[40], 339[67]; V, 4[5iv], 376–78[159]; 1993–2014: IV, 201–202[40], 243[67]; V, 311–13[159]; VII, 262[254]; Davies 2014: 243–44[40], 286–87[67].

83 Kitchen 1968–90: V, 378–80[160]; VII, 273–74[258]; 1993–2014: V, 313–14[160]; VII, 188[258].

84 oBerlin P10633 (Kitchen 1968–90: V, 529–30[224 A.148]; 1993–2014: V, 417[224 A.148]).

85 pTurin C1891 (Kitchen 1968–90: IV, 76–77[56]; 1993–2014: IV, 70–71[56]).

86 Cf. Kruchten 1979.

87 Kitchen 1968–90: IV, 364–65[31]; V, 2[3], 381[161]; 1993–2014: IV, 264[31]; V, 2[3], 315[161]; Davies 2014: 321[31]; Dodson 2016a: 130.

88 Kitchen 1968–90: V, 381–83[162]; VI, 79–81[59]; VII, 274[259]; 1993–2014: V, 315–16[162]; VI, 73–74[59]; VII, 189[259].

89 Kitchen 1968–90: V, 384–84[163]; VII, 275–76[260]; 1993–2014: V, 316–17[163]; VII, 189–90[260].

90 Kitchen 1968–90: V, 384–90[165]; 1993–2014: V, 317–21[165].

91 Kitchen 1968–90: V, 391–92[166–68]; 1993–2014: V, 321–23[166–68].

92 Kitchen 1968–90: V, 392–97[169–78]; 1993–2014: V, 323–26[169–78].

93 Kitchen 1968–90: V, 7[11], 397–99 [179]; 1993–2014: V, 327–28[179]; VII, 179–80; Roberson 2018: 71–72[199].

94 Kitchen 1968–90: V, 505[221 l.15]; 1993–2014: V, 401[221 l.15].

95 Kitchen 1968–90: V, 399[180]; VI, 12[9], 87–90[68], 91–92[69.1.c], 93[69.1.e], 518–19[Doc. B]; 1993–2014: V, 329[180]; VI, 12[9], 7[68], 82–83[69.1.c], 83–84[69.1.e], 385[Doc. B].

96 His younger son, Amenhotep G, was a key figure in the upheavals of the late Twentieth Dynasty, and may have been the father of Nesibanebdjedet I and father-in-law of Herihor (see Dodson 2019a: 38).

97 Kitchen 1968–90: V, 400–12[181]; VII, 280–81[265]; 1993–2014: V, 323–41[181]; VII, 192–94[265].

98 Kitchen 1968–90: V, 412–14[182]; VI, 90–94[69], 233–34[C.XVI.1]; 1993–2014: V, 341–42[182]; VI, 81–84[69], 181–82[C.XVI.1].

99 Kitchen 1968–90: V, 427–29[202–203, 205]; 1993–2014: V, 353–55[202–203, 205].

100 pWilbour [pBrooklyn 34.5596.4], A34, 49 (Gardiner 1941–52: I, pl. 16; II, 145; III, 36).

101 Pahemnetjer and Hori I are shown together on the double statue Louvre A72 (Kitchen 1968–90: IV, 294[XVIII.2]; 1993–2014: IV, 212[XVIII.2]; Davies 2014: 256).

102 Kitchen 1968–90: IV, 379–81[45]; 1993–2014: IV, 276–77[45]; Davies 2014: 336–37.

103 Dodson 2019a: 59.

104 UPMAA E13578 (Schulman 1960).

105 Kitchen 1968–90: VI, 523–24[26]; 1993–2014: VI, 387–88[26].

106 Although Schulman confidently identifies him with Rameses IX's vizier.

107 See Černý 1973; Valbelle 1985; Ventura 1986; Davies 1999 for data on Deir el-Medina from this period.

108 oTurin N.57036=S5660 (Kitchen 1968–90: V, 496[A.94]; 1993–2014: V, 394[A.94]).

109 oTurin N.57031=S5645 (Kitchen 1968–90: V, 503[A.103]; 1993–2014: V, 399[A.103]).

110 See Janssen 1975.

111 oChicago OI 16991 (Kitchen 1968–90: V, 559–60[228]; 1993–2014: V, 436–37[228]. Cf. Janssen 1979 on oTurin N.57072.

112 oBerlin P10633 (Kitchen 1968–90: V, 529–30[224 A.148]; 1993–2014: V, 416–17[224 A.148]). This also indicates that the temple was still operational, thus had probably not yet begun to be dismantled (cf. pp. 24–25).

113 For these events, see pTurin C1880 [the Turin Strike Papyrus] (Gardiner 1948: xiv–xvii, pl. 49–51; Frandsen 1990).

114   oDM36, l.9; oDM38, l.22 (Kitchen 1968–90: V, 548, 552; 1993–2014: V, 428, 431).

Notes to Chapter 3

1   Royal princes had held such offices as the vizierate during the Fourth Dynasty, while a few had held senior priestly posts during the Eighteenth Dynasty (see Dodson 1990).

2   Kitchen 1968–90: II, 858–63[III]; 1993–2014: II, 559–63[III]; 1999: 571–75[III].

3   Porter and Moss 1972: 273; for the key discussion of her identity, see Černý 1958.

4   Cairo CG42153 (Porter and Moss 1972: 143).

5   Porter and Moss 1960–64: 613.

6   Porter and Moss 1960–64: 756; Thomas 1966: 223; Leblanc 1989: pl. cvii–cxiii.

7   E.g. Tawosret's KV14, begun when she was wife of Sethy II.

8   Porter and Moss 1960–64: 756–58; Thomas 1966: 223–24; Leblanc 1989: pl. cxiv–cxxvi.

9   Schiaparelli 1924: 155–56; Bruyère 1952: 31–32.

10   Grist 1985.

11   Kitchen 1984; Dodson 1987.

12   Collier, Dodson, and Hamernik 2010.

13   Abitz 1986.

14   Porter and Moss 1960–64: 500; Thomas 1966: 150–51.

15   oBerlin P10663 (Wente 1973; Kitchen 1968–90: V, 558–59[A.204]; 1993–2004: V, 436[A.204]).

16   Porter and Moss 1960–64: 752–53; Thomas 1966: 219–20; Leblanc 1989: pl. lxxxiii–lxxxviii.

17   Fisher 2001: I, 81–89; II, 84–89.

18   Porter and Moss 1960–64: 759–61; Thomas 1966: 221–22; Leblanc 1989: pl. cxxxiii–cxliv.

19   For their homonym under Rameses II, the latter's eldest son, see Fisher 2001: I, 43–70; II, 63–78.

20   Porter and Moss 1960–64: 759; Thomas 1966: 221; Leblanc 1989: pl. cxxvii–cxxxi.

21   Also borne by Rameses II's second son (Fisher 2001: I, 71–80; II, 78–84).

22   Thomas 1966: 220.

23   Seele 1955: 303–304, 312–13.

24   Porter and Moss 1960–64: 753–54; Thomas 1966: 220–21.

25   The name Sethhirkopeshef was apparently one used by Rameses II's eldest son, Amenhirkopeshef, during the latter part of his life (see the discussion in Fisher 2001: I, 58–61).

26   Porter and Moss 1960–64: 754–55; Thomas 1966: 221; Leblanc 1989: pl. xci–cv; Hassanein and Nelson 1997.

27   For its history, and a full discussion, see Kitchen 1982.

28   For a discussion of the title, see Fisher 2001: I, 62–63.

29   Kitchen 1968–90: V, 412[182(1bi)]; 1993–2004: V, 341[182(1bi)].

30   On the other hand, Susan Redford (2002: 40) finds this "puzzling" and suggests that the first figure had been intended to be another son—the Pentaweret who was involved in the murder of Rameses III (see further below).

31   For Montjuhirkopeshef A, the fifth son of Rameses II and also a First Charioteer, see Fisher 2001: I, 107; II, 143–45.

32   For the homonymous sixteenth son of Rameses II, and also Heliopolitan pontiff, see Fisher 2001: I, 117–18; II, 171–77.

33   For the seventh son of Rameses II, see Fisher 2001: I, 108; II, 147–49.

34   Kitchen 1968–90: V, 373–74[156], 375[157B]; 1993–2014: V, 309–10[156], 311[157B]; Leblanc 2001; 2001–2002.

35   Porter and Moss 1960–64: 546; Thomas 1966: 151–52.

36   Brock 2013: 101–108.

37   For which see Dodson 2016a: 107–10.

38   Altenmüller 1994a.

39   On the Montjuhirkopeshef question, cf. Altenmüller 1994b.

40   Kitchen 1968–90: V, 114[43(v)]; 1993–2004: V, 80[43(v)].

41   Kitchen 1968–90: V, 372[155(2i)]; 1993–2004: V, 309[155(2i)].

42   Florence 4019 (Kitchen 1968–90: V, 373[155(2ii3)]; 1993–2004: V, 309[155(2ii3)]).

43   Kitchen 1968–90: V, 373[155(6)]; 1993–2004: V, 309[155(6)].

44   Luxor Museum.

45   Susan Redford's implicit denial of this (2002: 40–42) on the basis of the fact that he is Generalissimo of infantry, rather than bowmen, seems rather forced, especially as the form of the soldier hieroglyph is unclear in many of Rameses C's extant titularies—and in at least one case (the games scene at Medinet Habu) is certainly not a bowman (see Epigraphic Survey 1932: 112).

46   Susan Redford would see him as Rameses C, and the upper figure as the "unknown" prince; but see previous note.

47   The overseer of her harem was one Amenhotep (TT346—Kitchen 1968–90: VI, 86[65]).

48   Porter and Moss 1960–64: 767–88; Thomas 1966: 218; Leblanc 1989: pl. cxciii–cc.

49   For example, Iset E, daughter of Rameses VI, and also God's Wife of Amun (Kitchen 1968–90: VI, 282[9], 321–22[16], 347–48[III]; 1993–2014: VI, 214[9], 257[16], 273–74[III]).

50   Peden 1994: 5–6.

51   pTurin C1875 [Turin Judicial Papyrus]; pBibNat 195 [pRollin 1888]; pLee (PML Amh. Egy. Pap. 5.1–2); pRifaud (Kitchen 1968–90: V, 350–66[148–50]; 1993–2014: V, 297–305[148–50]).

pVarzy (Varzy [Nièvre], Musée Auguste Grasset) seems now not to form part of the archive (Loffet and Matoïan 1996). For discussions of the events, see Goedicke 1963; S. Redford 2002; Vernus 2003: 107–20.

52   Trusted members of the royal household, who were frequently used by kings for special commissions.

53   Further confusion has been caused by the practice of using 'harem' to translate both ipt (nswt) and ḫnr, the latter apparently originating as a musical troupe, although having close links with the ipt by the New Kingdom (see Callender 1994).

54   Kanawati 2003; Vernus 2003.

55   Kitchen 1968–90: II, 858–68[319–25]; 1993–2014: II: 559–63[319–25]; 1999: 571–75.

56   This being the day before the announcement of the king's death and the accession of Rameses IV, as recorded in pTurin C1949+1946 (Kitchen 1968–90: V, 557[A.202]; 1993–2014: V, 435[A.202]).

57   pTurin C1875, §5:7.

58   pTurin C1875, §4:2.

59   See Dodson 2016a: 35–37.

60   pBibNat 195, l.1–2.

61   Goedicke 1963.

62   pTurin C1875, §6:1.

63   Schott 1953.

64   As argued by Goedicke 1963: 84–87.

65   oDM40, rt. 14–15 (Kitchen 1968–90: VI, 107[A.9]; 1993–2014: VI, 93[A.9]).

66   As in the context of another potentially disputed succession, the depiction of Ay burying Tutankhamun on the wall of the latter's burial chamber.

Notes to Chapter 4

1   For an overview of Egyptian tombs and their development over time, see Dodson and Ikram 2008.

2   For a survey of royal funerary monuments over time, see Dodson 2016b.

3   Porter and Moss 1972: 481–527; Murnane 1980; Weeks 2001: 96–109.

4   Hornung 1991.

5   Porter and Moss 1960–64: 564–65.

6   On the odd layout of the latter, see Mauric-Barbiero 2003; Hovestreydt 2014: 109.

7   For an overview and discussion of these rooms, see Hovestreydt 2014.

8   See Baines 1985: 175–80, 378.

9   J.G. Wilkinson 1835: 113, stating that "[e]ach of these small apartments has a pit, now closed, in which it is probable that some of the officers of the king's household were buried; and the subjects on their walls will then refer to the station they held."

10   Hovestreydt 2014: 105 n.11.

11   Hovestreydt 2014: 125–26.

12   Hornung 1999.

13   The *Amduat* in the tomb of the vizier User (TT61), contemporary with the first royal use of the work under Hatshepsut and Thutmose III.

14   Montet 1947: pl. xxvi; during the previous dynasty, Panedjem I had possessed a full Book of the Dead papyrus, including the weighing of the heart and the Fields of Iaru (Cairo SR11488 [Saleh and Sourouzian 1987: [235]]).

15   Cf. R.H. Wilkinson 1995: 79–81.

16   See Dodson 2016c: 253–56.

17   Porter and Moss 1960–64: 526.

18   Dodson 1986a.

19   Dodson 1986b.

20   Mojsov 1991–92.

21   Personal communication, Lyla Pinch-Brock, 12 December 2018.

22   Porter and Moss 1960–64: 555; Piacentini and Orsenigo 2004: 127, 176–77.

23   Personal communication, the late Edwin C. Brock.

24   Dodson 1994: 51–53.

25   Dodson 1996.

26   Aubert and Aubert 1974: 116.

27   Louvre AF425 (Bovot 2003: 174–76[69]).

28   OIM E10705, E10755; BM EA8695, EA67816.

29   Louvre N656A, N656B; Turin C2507; BM EA33938; Durham N1832.

30   Clayton 1972.

31   As known from the time of Thutmose III down to at least that of Rameses IX.

32   Actually statues of the king and his *ka*, as known from the tombs of Tutankhamun (Cairo JE60707–8), Horemheb (Cairo JE46888, 46944, 55331), Rameses I (BM EA854, EA883), and Rameses IX (BM EA882).

Notes to Chapter 5

1   This temple, perhaps begun late in the reign, lay on the Asasif, and was later continued by Rameses V and then Rameses VI, but never finished (Porter and Moss 1972: 424–26). Rameses IV also began two other West Theban temples, one a little to the north of the 'great' temple, around the end of his first regnal year (Porter and Moss 1972: 424), and another just north of Medinet Habu (Porter and Moss 1972: 454): how these never-finished buildings relate to each other remains unclear.

2   Kitchen 1968–90: VI, 17–20[15]; 1993–2014: VI, 18–21[15]; for an overview of the reign of Rameses IV, see Peden 1994.

3   Kitchen 1968–90: VI, 278[1]; 1993–2014: VI, 211[1].

4   Kitchen 1984.

5   For the last years of the Twentieth Dynasty, see Dodson 2019a: 3–38.

6   For these documents, see Peet 1930.

7   pBM EA10052: 1.18 (Kitchen 1968–90: VI, 768–69[25]; 1993–2014: VI, 540[25]; for the translation of the items stolen, see Cooney 2007: 18–21, 22–28), and on the fate of the material stolen, see Davies 2017–18.

8   pBM EA10052: 6.22–23 (Collier, Dodson, and Hamernik 2010).

9   The robbery is recorded in pMayer B [pLiverpool M.11186] (Kitchen 1968–90: VI, 515–16[25]; 1993–2014: VI, 383–84[25]), with the date derived from a graffito on the ceiling of the burial chamber of KV9 (Kitchen 1968–90: VI, 658–59[A.24]; 1993–2014: VI, 467[A.24]; Barwik 2011: 24–29).

10   Cairo CG61021 (Porter and Moss 1960–64: 661).

11   Reeves 1990: 169, 230, 235, 248.

12   Personal communication, Donald P. Ryan, 4 January 2019.

13   For example, Rameses I, Sethy I, and Rameses II (see Dodson 2019b: 113–14).

14   See Aston 2013; 2015.

15   The mummy of Panedjem's son-in-law(?) Djedptahiufankh had bandages dated to Shoshenq's Year 11, while that of his wife(?) Nesitanebetashru included a bandage with an unattributed Year 13.

16   On the chronology of the movements of the royal mummies and their final deposition, see Reeves 1990, superseding all earlier treatments.

17   Cairo CG61003 (Porter and Moss 1960–64: 659).

18   Such "Libyans" are frequently noted in the contemporary documents from Deir el-Medina.

19   Hölscher 1954: 36–44.

20   Baillet 1926: II, 523–27.

21   For the Valley in Greco-Roman times, see Coppens 2016.

22   Owing to Rameses VI sharing his prenomen with Amenhotep III, one of whose colossal statues had by then been identified as representing the Greek hero Memnon.

23   Hölscher 1954: 45–57; Wilfong 2002.

Notes to Chapter 6

1   Although there was continuing local interest in them: see El Daly 2005.

2   Bierbrier 2012: 438–39.

3   Pococke 1743: 99.

4   Pococke 1743: 106.

5   Bierbrier 2012: 83.

6   Bruce 1790: 125–26.

7   Bierbrier 2012: 52–53.

8   Belzoni 1820: 373–74.

9   See Hornung 1990: 120–27, pl. 89–93.

10   Bruce 1790: 126–34.

11   Browne 1799: 137–38.

12   Jomard 1809–28: A.II, pl. 78.

13   Jomard 1809–28: A.II, pl. 84[7], 85[1–5, 5, 6, 10–13], 86–91.

14   Jomard 1809–28: A.II, pl. 2–4, 6–17.

15   English edition Denon 1803: II, 96–97.

16   Bierbrier 2012: 484–85.

17   See Dodson 2019b: 123–32.

18   Bickerstaffe 2006; this piece (BM EA78) was long confused with the lid of the sarcophagus of Rameses III, with consequent distortions of the chronology of Belzoni's activities; the following narrative follows Bickerstaffe's conclusions.

19   Bierbrier 2012: 161–62.

20   Belzoni 1820: 250.

21   Manley and Rée 2001: 151; Bickerstaffe (2006: 27–28) questions whether Salt was aware of the precise tomb from which the lid came, on the basis that Salt would surely have wanted to keep it together with the coffer.

22   Bierbrier 2012: 28.

23   D'Athanasi 1836: 52; but see pp. 127–28, above, on the identity of the sarcophagus described by Bruce.

24   Manley and Rée 2001: 197–208.

25   Bierbrier 2012: 114–15.

26   Manley and Rée 2001: 243–45.

27   Louvre D1.

28   See Dodson 2019b: 132–35.

29   Belzoni 1822: 5.

30   For the acquisition of the lid, see Wilson 2002.

31   Bierbrier 2012: 59–60.

32   Personal communication, Janine Bourriau, 1987.

33   Bierbrier 2012: 96–97.

34   Bierbrier 2012: 579–80.

35   Bierbrier 2012: 307–308.

36   Bierbrier 2012: 246–47.

37   Wilkinson employed a few vignettes in his later popular publications; Lane's entire account was finally published in 2000. Some of Hay's sketches from chamber J of the tomb were published by Mauric-Barberio in 2004.

38   Thompson 2015: 165–70.

39   Bierbrier 2012: 473.

40   Amenmeses, Siptah, and Tawosret had not yet been placed: Wilkinson (and Champollion and Rosellini) relied on the Festival of Min reliefs at Medinet Habu, which 'edited out' these three rulers. Siptah was, however, recognized as being posterior to "Amunmai Rameses" (Rameses II), with Amenmeses regarded as "probably posterior to the nineteenth dynasty" and Tawosret (as queen) before Siptah (J.G. Wilkinson 1828–30: 119).

41   J.G. Wilkinson 1828–30: 94–95.

42   See Rosellini 1832–44: I/2, 252–78.

43   Rosellini 1832–44: I/2, 259; he places Amenmeses between his "Ramses XII" (Rameses XI) and "Ramses XIII" (Rameses V).

44   Rosellini 1832–44: I/2, 5.

45   In Champollion 1835–45 and Rosellini 1832–44, with one in Champollion 1844–89.

46   In Champollion 1844–89.

47   Weber 2018.

48   J.G. Wilkinson 1835: 50–76.

49   Lepsius 1849–59; 1897–1913.

50   Bierbrier 2012: 324–26.

51   Coming to the throne in 1293 (Bunsen 1848–67: IV, 526).

52   Bunsen 1848–67: III, 79–80.

53   Bunsen 1848–67: III, 232.

54   Grandet 1994: I, 1–18.

55   Hamernik 2010: 238–39.

56   Bierbrier 2012: 243.

57   Bierbrier 2012: 175.

58   Eisenlohr 1872a; 1872b; the 'historical' part was also considered by François Chabas (1817–82 [Bierbrier 2012: 112–13]) in 1873.

59   Bierbrier 2012: 244.

60   Following preliminary treatments in 1872–73.

61   Eisenlohr and Birch 1876; a definitive transcription of the papyrus into hieroglyphs was published by Wolja Erichsen in 1933, and an exhaustive study, with a fully annotated translation into French, by Pierre Grandet in 1994; the only full translation into English remains that of James H. Breasted, published in 1906.

62   Devéria 1865–67.

63   Renouf 1876.

64   Bierbrier 2012: 2.

65   For the story of the discovery of TT320 and a discussion of the many issues involved, see Bickerstaffe 2010.

66   Bierbrier 2012: 83–84.

67   Bierbrier 2012: 288.

68   Bierbrier 2012: 359–61.

69   Alongside another mummy of "rather poor" appearance; this had been one of

the female bodies given an "emergency" unwrapping in 1885 (see Maspero 1889: 535–36).

70   Maspero 1889: 563–66[20], translated from the French by the author.

71   Bierbrier 2012: 42–43.

72   Bierbrier 2012: 197.

73   Bierbrier 2012: 75–76.

74   Bierbrier 2012: 273.

75   Given that only the head was freed from the carapace, clearly no close examination of the genital region took place. The comment was presumably made on the absence of any obvious bulge in the area; however, the organs have now been identified by modern imaging work (Hawass and Saleem 2016: 184–86).

76   For example, Peden 1994: 12 n.6; S. Redford 2002: 106.

77   Bierbrier 2012: 515–16.

78   G.E. Smith 1912: 87.

79   For more detail on the modern history of the royal mummies, see Ikram 2017 and Dodson 2019b: 144–49.

80   Coury 1992.

81   Bierbrier 2012: 338; for the discovery, see Piacentini and Orsenigo 2004.

82   Bierbrier 2012: 318.

83   Lefébure 1886–89: II, 87–120.

84   For example, the 1818 flood in Sethy I's KV17 (Belzoni 1820: 370–71).

85   Thomas 1966: 110; Weber 2018.

86   For example, J.G. Wilkinson 1837: 61; some injudicious tinting of a copy (Prisse d'Avennes 1878–79: II, pl. [52]) of one of the images of Tyti in the tomb later led Wallis Budge (1902: 96) to proclaim Tiye as possessing "a fair complexion and blue eyes," and thus a North Syrian.

87   Bunsen 1848–67: II, 539–42.

88   Reported in Lefébure 1885: 126.

89   Bierbrier 2012: 53–54.

90   Bierbrier 2012: 492–93.

91   Schiaparelli 1924.

92   Bierbrier 2012: 102–103.

93   Campbell 1909.

94   Cf. Epigraphic Survey 1930: ix–x.

95   Bierbrier 2012: 78–79.

96   Abt 2011: 281.

97   Bierbrier 2012: 96.

98   Bierbrier 2012: 145–46; Adams 2013.

99   Burton 1916; cf. Murnane 1980: 69; Adams 2013: 297–98.

100 Bierbrier 2012: 401.

101 Bierbrier 2012: 470.

102 Abt 2011: 281–301.

103 Bierbrier 2012: 261–62.

104 Epigraphic Survey 1930; 1932; Edgerton and Wilson 1936.

105 Cf. Johnson 2010.

106 Bierbrier 2012: 392–93.

107 Bierbrier 2012: 320–21.

108 Bierbrier 2012: 434–35.

109 Kitchen 1968–90: V, 8–671; 1993–2014: 9–508.

110 Kitchen 1968–90: VII, 259–324, 415–16; 1993–2014: 180–218.

111 Roberson 2018: 73–103.

112 Harris and Weeks 1973: 47, 164; Harris and Wente 1980: 172, 290, 294.

113 Harris and Wente 1980: 333.

114 Harris and Wente 1980: 188–212.

115 S. Redford 2002: 107.

116 Cf. Robins 1981.

117 Reeve and Adams 1993; Molleson and Cox 1993.

118 Hawass et al. 2012; Hawass and Saleem 2016: 179–91.

119 Hawass and Saleem 2016: 181–82.

120 Hawass and Saleem 2016: 190–91.

121 Cairo CG61098 (Maspero 1889: 548–51; G.E. Smith 1912: 114–16; Brier 2006a; 2006b).

122 Cf. Bickerstaffe's remarks on the extraction of reliable samples, and the failure to include the mummy of Rameses

III's undoubted sons Rameses IV and VI in the comparison (2018: 30).

123   Weber 2018.

124   **Andrzejewski 1962.**

125   Bierbrier 2012: 21.

126   Hornung 1963; 1975–77.

127   **Marciniak 1982; 1983.**

128   Weber 2018; www.ramesses-iii-project. com/english/the-project/.

129   For comprehensive coverage of the issue of historicity of Rameses III's documents, and especially the Medinet Habu reliefs, see James 2017; see also D.B. Redford 2018: 95–112.

130   Bierbrier 2012: 237–38.

131   For example, Gardiner 1961: 282 (Nubia, following Säve-Söderbergh 1941: 173–74), 288 (Syria).

132   Lesko 1980; cf. also Lesko 1992.

133   Kitchen 1991: 238.

134   Strobel 2011.

135   Kitchen 2012: 16.

136   Kahn 2010: 20 n.45.

137   Kahn 2010: 16.

138   Kitchen 2012: 12.

139   Kahn 2011: 4; 2015; 2016; 2018; D.B. Redford 2018: 142, echoing some comments made by Simons back in 1937.

140   Kitchen 2012: 16, contra Cifola 1991

141   In addition to the 'mainstream' attempts at reassessing Rameses III discussed just above, one should also note more radical ones that reset his place in history via the so-called 'New Chronology.' The latter proposes the reduction of the chronology of the Late Bronze Age by a matter of centuries, one variant (as set out in James 1991) lowering New Kingdom dates by some 250 years, and placing Rameses III in the late tenth century BC. A concomitant of this has been to equate Rameses III with "Shishak, King of Egypt," whom the Old Testament cites as having plundered Jerusalem in Year 5 of King Rehoboam of Judah, rather than his conventional equation with Shoshenq I of the Twenty-second Dynasty (see also James and Van der Veen 2015). Leaving aside the many other problems of the 'New Chronology' (cf. my initial comments in Dodson 1992), it has been pointed out that while the equivalence of 'Shishak' and 'Shoshenq' is fairly transparent, there seems no credible way in which 'Rameses' could be transmogrified into 'Shishak' (Sagrillo 2015). This is also the case with the other principal variant of the 'New Chronology' (for which see Rohl 1995), which requires 'Shishak' to be Rameses II.

BIBLIOGRAPHY

Abbreviations for Periodicals

AncEg   *Ancient Egypt* (Manchester: Ancient Egypt Magazine).

ASAE   *Annales du Service des Antiquités de l'Égypte* (Cairo: Institut français d'archéologie orientale/Supreme Council of Antiquities Press.

BACE   *Bulletin of the Australian Centre for Egyptology* (Sydney: Australian Centre for Egyptology).

BES   *Bulletin of the Egyptological Seminar* (New York: Egyptological Seminar of New York).

BIFAO   *Bulletin de l'Institut français d'archéologie orientale* (Cairo: Institut français d'archéologie orientale).

BMMA   *Bulletin of Metropolitan Museum of Art* (New York: Metropolitan Museum of Art).

CAJ   *Cambridge Archaeological Journal* (Cambridge: Cambridge University Press).

DE   *Discussions in Egyptology* (Oxford: DE Publications).

GM   *Göttinger Miszellen* (Göttingen: Universität Göttingen. Ägyptologisches Seminar).

JAEI   *Journal of Ancient Egyptian Interconnections* (Tucson: University of Arizona).

JARCE   *Journal of the American Research Center in Egypt* (New York: American Research Center in Egypt).

JEA   *Journal of Egyptian Archaeology* (London: Egypt Exploration Fund/Society).

JNES   *Journal of Near Eastern Studies* (Chicago: University of Chicago Press).

JSSEA   *Journal of the Society for the Study of Ancient Egypt* (Toronto: Society for the Study of Ancient Egypt).

MDAIK   *Mitteilungen des Deutschen Archäologischen Instituts, Kairo* (Mainz: Philipp von Zabern).

MMJ   *Metropolitan Museum Journal* (New York: Metropolitan Museum of Art).

OJA   *Oxford Journal of Archaeology* (Oxford: Basil Blackwell).

RdE   *Revue d'Egyptologie* (Leuven: Peeters).

RevArch   *Revue Archéologique* (Paris: Ernest Leroux).

SAK   *Studien zur altägyptschen Kultur* (Hamburg: H. Buske Verlag).

TSBA   *Transactions of the Society of Biblical Archaeology* (London: Society of Biblical Archaeology).

ZÄS   *Zeitschrift für ägyptische Sprache und Altertumskunde* (Leipzig: J.C. Hinrichs/ Berlin: Akademie Verlag).

Works Cited

Abitz, F. 1986. *Ramses III: in den Gräbern seiner Söhne*. Freiburg: Universitätsverlag/ Göttingen: Vandenhoeck & Ruprecht.

Abt, J. 2011. *American Egyptologist: The Life of James Henry Breasted and the Creation of His Oriental Institute*. Chicago: University of Chicago.

Adams, J.M. 2013. *The Millionaire and the Mummies: Theodore Davis's Gilded Age in the Valley of the Kings*. New York: St. Martin's Press.

Altenmüller, H. 1994a. "Dritter Vorbericht in die Arbeiten des Archäologischen Instituts der Universität Hamburg am Grab des Bay (KV13) im Tal der Könige von Theben." *SAK* 21: 1–18.

———. 1994b. "Prinz Mentu-her-chopeschef aus der 20. Dynastie." *MDAIK* 50: 1–12.

Andrzejewski, T. 1962. "Le Livre des portes dans la salle du sarcophage du tombeau de Ramsès III." *ASAE* 57: 1–6.

Aston, D.A. 2013. "TT 320 and the ḫ3y of Queen Inhapi—A Reconsideration Based on Ceramic Evidence." *GM* 236: 7–20.

———. 2015. "TT 358, TT 320, and KV 39: Three Early Eighteenth Dynasty Queen's Tombs in the Vicinity of Deir el-Bahri." In *Deir el-Bahari Studies: Special Studies*, edited by Z. Szafranski, 14–42. Warsaw: Polish Centre of Mediterranean Archaeology.

Aubert, J.-F., and L. Aubert. 1974. *Statuettes égyptiennes: chaouabtis, ouchebtis*. Paris: Librairie d'Amérique et d'Orient Adrien Maisonneuve.

Baillet, J. 1926. *Inscriptions grecques et latines des tombeaux des rois ou syringes à Thèbes*. 2 vols. Cairo: Institut français d'archéologie orientale.

Baines, J. 1985. *Fecundity Figures: Egyptian Personification and the Iconology of a Genre*. Warminster: Aris and Phillips.

Barwik, M. 2011. *The Twilight of Ramesside Egypt: Studies on the History of Egypt at the End of the Ramesside Period*. Warsaw: Agade.

Belzoni, G. 1820. *Narrative of the Operations and Recent Discoveries within the Pyramids, Temples, Tombs and Excavations in Egypt and Nubia*. London: John Murray.

———. 1822. *Catalogue of the Various Articles of Antiquity, to Be Disposed of, at the Egyptian Tomb, by Auction, or by Private Contract*. London: William Clowes.

Ben-Dor Evian, S. 2016. "The Battles between Ramesses III and the 'Sea-Peoples': When, Where and Who? An Iconic Analysis of the Egyptian Reliefs." *ZÄS* 143: 151–68.

———. 2017. "Ramesses III and the 'Sea-Peoples': Towards a New Philistine Paradigm." *OJA* 36: 267–85.

Bénédite, G. 1894. "Le tombeau de la reine Thiti." In *Mémoires publiés par les membres de la Mission archéologique française au Caire* 5/3: 381–412. Paris: Georges Leroux.

Bickerstaffe, D. 2006. "Strong Man—Wrong Tomb: The Problem of Belzoni's Sarcophagi." *AncEg* 6/6: 22–30.

———. 2010. "The History of the Discovery of the Cache." In *The Royal Cache TT 320: A Re-examination*, edited by E. Graefe and G. Belova, 13–36. Cairo: Supreme Council of Antiquities Press.

———. 2018. "'I'm Not Pentawere!' Screams 'Unknown Man E.'" *AncEg* 18/6: 26–30.

Bierbrier, M.L., ed. 2012. *Who Was Who in Egyptology*. 4th ed. London: Egypt Exploration Society.

Birch, S. 1876. *Facsimile of an Egyptian Hieratic Papyrus of the Reign of Rameses III, Now in the British Museum*. London: British Museum.

———. 1879. "On the Cover of the Sarcophagus of Rameses III, Now in the Fitzwilliam

Museum." *Cambridge Antiquarian Communications* 3: 371–78.

Bongrani, L. 1997. "The Punt Expedition of Ramses IIIrd: Considerations on the Report from the Papyrus Harris I." In *L'impero ramesside: convegno internazionale in onore di Sergio Donadoni*, 45–59. Rome: Università degli Studi di Roma.

Bovot, J.-L. 2003. *Les serviteurs funéraires royaux et princiers de l'Ancienne Égypte*. Paris: Réunion des Musées Nationaux.

Breasted, J.H. 1906. *Ancient Records of Egypt: Historical Documents from the Earliest Times to the Persian Conquest*. Vol. 4. Chicago: University of Chicago Press.

Brier, B. 2006a. "The Mummy of Unknown Man E: A Preliminary Re-examination." *Bulletin of the Egyptian Museum* 3: 23–32.

———. 2006b. "The Mystery of Unknown Man E." *Archaeology* 59: 36–42.

Brock, E.C. 2013. "Some Observations on the Valley of the Kings in the Twentieth Dynasty." In *Archaeological Research in the Valley of the Kings and Ancient Thebes: Papers Presented in Honor of Richard H. Wilkinson*, edited by P.P. Creasman, 101–22. Tucson: University of Arizona Egyptian Expedition.

Browne, W.G. 1799. *Travels in Africa, Egypt and Syria, from the Year 1792 to 1798*. London: T. Cadell Junior & W. Davies/T.N. Longman & O. Rees.

Bruce, J. 1790. *Travels to Discover the Source of the Nile, in the Years 1768, 1769, 1770, 1771, 1772, and 1773*. 5 vols. London: C.C.J. and J. Robinson.

Brugsch, H. 1879. *Dictionnaire géographique de l'ancienne Égypte*. Leipzig: J.C. Hinrichs.

Bruyère, B. 1952. "Nebnerou et Hery-mâat." *BIFAO* 53: 31–32.

Bryce, T. 1998. *The Kingdom of the Hittites*. Oxford: Clarendon Press.

Budge, E.A.W. 1902. *A History of Egypt from the End of the Neolithic Period to the Death of Cleopatra VII, B.C. 30*. 6 vols. London: Kegan Paul, Rench, Trübner.

Bunbury, J.M., A. Graham, and M.A. Hunter. 2008. "Stratigraphic Landscape Analysis: Charting the Holocene Movements of the Nile at Karnak through Ancient Egyptian Time." *Geoarchaeology: An International Journal* 23/3: 351–73.

Bunsen, C.C.J. 1848–67. *Egypt's Place in Universal History*. 5 vols. London: Longman, Brown, Green, Longmans, & Roberts.

Burton, H. 1916. "The Late Theodore M. Davis's Excavations at Thebes in 1912–13: II. Excavations at Medinet Habu." *BMMA* 11/5: 102–108.

Callender, G. 1994. "The Nature of the Egyptian 'Harem,' Dynasties 1–20." *BACE* 5: 7–10.

Campbell, C. 1909. *Two Theban Queens, Nefert-ari and Ty-ti, and Their Tombs*. London: Kegan Paul, Trench, Trübner & Co.

Černý, J. 1958. "Queen Ēse of the Twentieth Dynasty and Her Mother." *JEA* 44: 31–37.

———. 1973. *A Community of Workmen at Thebes in the Ramesside Period*. Cairo: Institut français d'archéologie orientale.

Chabas, F.J. 1872. *Étude sur l'antiquité historique d'après les sources égyptiennes et les monuments réputés préhistoriques*. Châlon-sur-Saône: Dejussieu/Paris: Maisonneuve.

———. 1873. *Recherches pour servir à l'histoire de la XIXme dynastie et spécialement à celle des temps de l'Exode*. Châlon-sur-Saône: Dejussieu/Paris: Maisonneuve.

Champollion, J.-F. 1835–45. *Monuments de l'Égypte et de la Nubie: planches*. 4 vols. Paris: Firmin Didot Frères.

———. 1844–89. *Monuments de l'Égypte et de la Nubie: notices descriptives conformes aux manuscrits autographes*. 2 vols. Paris: Firmin Didot Frères.

Christophe, L.-A. 1953. "Les fondations de Ramsès III entre Memphis et Thèbes." *Cahiers d'histoire égyptienne* 5/4: 227–49.

Cifola, B. 1991. "The Terminology of Ramses III's Historical Records with a Formal Analysis of the War Scenes." *Orientalia* NS 60: 9–57.

Clayton, P.A. 1972. "Royal Bronze Shawabti Figures." *JEA* 58: 167–75.

Cline, E.H. 2014. *1177 B.C.: The Year Civilization Collapsed*. Princeton, NJ: Princeton University Press.

Cline, E.H., and D. O'Connor. 2003. "The Mystery of the 'Sea Peoples.'" In *Mysterious Lands*, edited by D. O'Connor and S. Quirke, 107–38. London: UCL Press.

———. 2012a. "The Sea Peoples." In *Ramesses III: The Life and Times of Egypt's Last Hero*, edited by E.H. Cline and D. O'Connor, 180–99. Ann Arbor: University of Michigan Press.

Cline, E.H., and D. O'Connor, eds. 2012b. *Ramesses III: The Life and Times of Egypt's Last Hero*. Ann Arbor: University of Michigan Press.

Collier, M., A. Dodson, and G. Hamernik. 2010. "P. BM EA 10052, Anthony Harris, and Queen Tyti." *JEA* 96: 242–47.

Cooney, K.M. 2007. *The Cost of Death: The Social and Economic Value of Ancient Egyptian Funerary Art in the Ramesside Period*. Leiden: Nederlands Instituut voor het Nabije Oosten.

Coppens, F. 2016. "Late Dynastic, Greco-Roman, and Christian Times: Post–New Kingdom Graffiti." In *The Oxford Handbook to the Valley of the Kings*, edited by R.H. Wilkinson and K.R. Weeks, 269–80. New York: Oxford University Press.

Coury, R.M. 1992. "The Politics of the Funereal: The Tomb of Saad Zaghlul." *JARCE* 29: 191–200.

Creasman, P.P., W.R. Johnson, J.B. McClain, and R.H. Wilkinson. 2014. "Foundation or Completion? The Status of Pharaoh-Queen Tausret's Temple of Millions of Years." *JNES* 77: 274–83.

El Daly, O. 2005. *Egyptology: The Missing Millennium: Ancient Egypt in Medieval Arabic Writings*. London: UCL.

Daressy, G. 1909. *Cerceuils des cachettes royales*. Cairo: Institut français d'archéologie orientale.

D'Athanasi, G. 1836. *A Brief Account of the Researches and Discoveries in Upper Egypt Made under the Direction of Henry Salt, Esq.* London: John Hearne.

Davies, B.G. 1999. *Who's Who at Deir el-Medina: A Prosopographic Study of the Royal Workmen's Community*. Leiden: Nederlands Instituut voor het Nabije Oosten.

———. 2014. *Ramesside Inscriptions: Translated and Annotated. Notes and Comments*. Vol. 4. Chichester: Wiley-Blackwell.

———. 2017–18. "The Ignominy of Deir el-Medina and the Cleansing of the Necropolis Workforce—A Re-examination of the Events of Year 17 of Ramesses IX." *JSSEA* 44: 159–81.

Denon, V. 1803. *Travels in Upper and Lower Egypt*. Translated by A. Aikin. 3 vols. London: T.N. Longman & O. Rees/Richard Phillips.

de Rougé, E. 1867. "Extraits d'un mémoire sur les attaques dirigées contre l'Egypte par les peuples de la Méditerranée vers le quatorzième siècle avant notre ère." *RevArch* NS 16: 35–45, 81–103.

Devéria, T. 1865–67. "Le papyrus judiciaire de Turin." *Journal asiatique* 6: 227–61, 331–77; 8: 154–95; 10: 402–76.

Dickinson, O.T.P.K. 2006. *The Aegean from Bronze Age to Iron Age: Continuity and Change between the Twelfth and Eighth Centuries BC*. London: Routledge.

Dodson, A. 1986a. "A Note on the Interior Decoration of the Coffer of the Sarcophagus of Ramesses III, Louvre D1 = N337." *DE* 5: 35.

———. 1986b. "Was the Sarcophagus of Ramesses III Begun for Sethos II?" *JEA* 72: 196–98.

———. 1987. "The Takhats and Some Other Royal Ladies of the Ramesside Period." *JEA* 73: 224–29.

———. 1990. "Crown Prince Djhutmose and the Royal Sons of the Eighteenth Dynasty." *JEA* 76: 87–96.

———. 1992. Review of James 1991. *Palestine Exploration Quarterly* Jan.–June: 71–72.

———. 1994. *The Canopic Equipment of the Kings of Egypt.* London: Kegan Paul International.

———. 1996. "A Canopic Jar of Ramesses IV and the Royal Canopic Equipment of the Ramesside Period." *GM* 152: 11–17.

———. 2016a. *Poisoned Legacy: The Fall of the Nineteenth Egyptian Dynasty.* Rev. ed. Cairo: American University in Cairo Press.

———. 2016b. *The Royal Tombs of Ancient Egypt.* Barnsley: Pen & Sword.

———. 2016c. "Sarcophagi." In *The Oxford Handbook of the Valley of the Kings*, edited by R.H. Wilkinson and K. Weeks, 245–59. Oxford: Oxford University Press.

———. 2018. *Amarna Sunset: Nefertiti, Tutankhamun, Ay, Horemheb, and the Egyptian Counter-Reformation.* 2nd ed. Cairo: American University in Cairo Press.

———. 2019a. *Afterglow of Empire: Egypt from the Fall of the New Kingdom to the Saite Renaissance.* 2nd ed. Cairo: American University in Cairo Press.

———. 2019b. *Sethy I, King of Egypt: His Life and Afterlife.* Cairo: American University in Cairo Press.

Dodson, A., and D. Hilton. 2010. *The Complete Royal Families of Ancient Egypt.* Paperback ed. London: Thames and Hudson.

Dodson, A., and S. Ikram. 2008. *The Tomb in Ancient Egypt: Royal and Private Sepulchres from the Early Dynastic Period to the Romans.* London: Thames & Hudson.

Edgerton, W.F., and J.A. Wilson. 1936. *Historical Records of Ramses III: The Texts in Medinet Habu.* 2 vols. Chicago: University of Chicago Press.

Eisenlohr, A. 1872a. *Der große Papyrus Harris: ein wichtiger Beitrag zur ägyptischen Geschichte,* ein 3000 Jahr altes Zeugniß für die mosaische Religionsstiftung enthaltend. Leipzig: J.C. Hinrichs.

———. 1872b. "On the Political Condition of Egypt before the Reign of Ramses III: Probably in Connection with the Establishment of the Jewish Religion, from the Great Harris Papyrus." *TSBA* 1: 355–84.

Eisenlohr, [A.], and S. Birch. 1876. "Annals of Rameses III: The Great Harris Papyrus." *Records of the Past* 6: 21–70; 8: 5–52. London: Society for Biblical Archaeology.

Epigraphic Survey. 1930. *Medinet Habu,* I: *Earlier Historical Records of Ramses III.* Chicago: University of Chicago Press.

———. 1932. *Medinet Habu,* II: *The Later Historical Records of Ramses III.* Chicago: University of Chicago Press.

———. 1934. *Medinet Habu,* III: *The Calendar, the "Slaughterhouse," and Minor Records of Ramses III.* Chicago: University of Chicago Press.

———. 1936a. *Reliefs and Inscriptions at Karnak,* I: *Ramses III's Temple within the Great Inclosure of Amon,* I. Chicago: University of Chicago Press.

———. 1936b. *Reliefs and Inscriptions at Karnak,* II: *Ramses III's Temple within the Great Inclosure of Amon,* II; *and Ramses III's Temple in the Precinct of Mut.* Chicago: University of Chicago Press.

———. 1940. *Medinet Habu,* IV: *Festival Scenes of Ramses III.* Chicago: University of Chicago Press.

———. 1957. *Medinet Habu,* V: *The Temple Proper,* I—*The Portico, the Treasury, and Chapels Adjoining the First Hypostyle Hall with Marginal Material from the Forecourts.* Chicago: University of Chicago Press.

———. 1963. *Medinet Habu,* VI: *The Temple Proper,* II—*The Re Chapel, the Royal Mortuary Complex, and Adjacent Rooms with Miscellaneous Material from the Pylons, the Forecourts, and the First Hypostyle Hall.* Chicago: University of Chicago Press.

———. 1964. *Medinet Habu*, VII: *The Temple Proper*, III—*The Third Hypostyle Hall and All Rooms Accessible from It with Friezes of Scenes from the Roof Terraces and Exterior Walls of the Temple*. Chicago: University of Chicago Press.

———. 1970. *Medinet Habu*, VIII: *The Eastern High Gate, with Translations of Texts*. Chicago: University of Chicago Press.

Erichsen, W. 1933. *Papyrus Harris I: Hieroglyphische Transkription*. Brussels: Fondation égyptologique Reine Élisabeth.

Fisher, M.M. 2001. *The Sons of Ramesses II*. 2 vols. Wiesbaden: Harrassowitz Verlag.

Frandsen, P.J. 1990. "Editing Reality: The Turin Strike Papyrus." In *Studies in Egyptology Presented to Miriam Lichtheim* 1, edited by S. Israelit-Groll, 166–99. Jerusalem: Magnes Press.

Freu, J. 1988. "La tablette RS86.2230 et la phase finale du royaume d'Ugarit." *Syria* 65: 395–98.

Gaballa, G.A. 1976. *Narrative in Egyptian Art*. Mainz: Philipp von Zabern.

Gardiner, A.H. 1910. "The Goddess Nekhbet at the Jubilee Festival of Rameses III." *ZÄS* 48: 47–51.

———, ed. 1941–52. *The Wilbour Papyrus*. 4 vols. Oxford: Oxford University Press for The Brooklyn Museum.

———. 1948. *Ramesside Administrative Documents*. London: Oxford University Press.

———. 1961. *Egypt of the Pharaohs: An Introduction*. Oxford: Clarendon Press.

Gardiner, A.H., and T.E. Peet. 1917. *The Inscriptions of Sinai*, I. London: Egypt Exploration Fund.

Goedicke, H. 1963. "Was Magic Used in the Harem Conspiracy against Ramesses III? (P.Rollin and P.Lee)." *JEA* 49: 71–92.

Grandet, P. 1993. *Ramsès III: histoire d'un règne*. Paris: Pygmalion/Gérard Watelet.

———. 1994. *Le papyrus Harris I (BM 9999)*. 2 vols. Cairo: Institut français d'archéologie orientale.

Grist, J. 1985. "The Identity of the Ramesside Queen Tyti." *JEA* 71: 71–81.

Hamernik, G. 2010. "On the Rediscovery of Anthony C. Harris's Books and Manuscripts at Alexandria." *JEA* 96: 236–42.

Harris, J.E., and K.R. Weeks. 1973. *X-Raying the Pharaohs*. London: Macdonald.

Harris, J.E., and E.F. Wente, eds. 1980. *An X-Ray Atlas of the Pharaohs*. Chicago: University of Chicago Press.

Hassanein, F., and M. Nelson. 1976. *La Tombe du Prince Amon-(Her)-Khepechef*. Cairo: Centre de documentation et d'études sur l'ancienne Égypte.

———. 1997. *La tombe du Prince Khaemouaset*. Cairo: Conseil Supérieur des Antiquités.

Hawass, Z., S. Ismail, A. Selim, S.N. Saleem, D. Fathalla, S. Wasef, A.Z. Gad, R. Saad, S. Fares, H. Amer, P. Gostner, Y.Z. Gad, C.M. Pusch, and A.R. Zink. 2012. "Revisiting the Harem Conspiracy and Death of Ramesses III: Anthropological, Forensic, Radiological, and Genetic Study." *British Medical Journal* 345/7888. doi: 10.1136/bmj.e8268.

Hawass, Z., and S.N. Saleem. 2016. *Scanning the Pharaohs: CT Imaging of the New Kingdom Royal Mummies*. Cairo: American University in Cairo Press.

Hayes, W.C. 1950. "The Sarcophagus of Sennemūt." *JEA* 36: 19–23.

Higginbotham, C. 1999. "The Statue of Ramses III from Beth Shean." *Tel Aviv* 26: 225–32.

Hölscher, U. 1910. *Das hohe Tor von Medinet Habu: eine baugeschichtliche Untersuchung*. Leipzig: Hinrichs.

———. 1941–51. *The Excavation of Medinet Habu*, III–IV: *The Mortuary Temple of Ramses III*. Chicago: University of Chicago Press.

———. 1954. *The Excavation of Medinet Habu, V: The Post-Ramessid Remains*. Chicago: University of Chicago Press.

Hornung, E. 1963. *Das Amduat: Die Schrift des verborgenen Raumes*. 2 vols. Wiesbaden: Harassowitz.

———. 1975–77. *Das Buch der Anbetung des Re im Westen (Sonnenlitanei): nach den Versionen des Neuen Reiches*. 2 vols. Geneva: Editions de Belles-Lettres.

———. 1990. *Zwei Ramessidische Königsgräber: Ramses IV. und Ramses VII*. Mainz: Philipp von Zabern.

———. 1991. *The Tomb of Pharaoh Seti I/Das Grab Sethos' I*. Zurich and Munich: Artemis.

———. 1999. *The Ancient Egyptian Books of the Afterlife*. Translated by David Lorton. Ithaca, NY: Cornell University Press.

———. 2006. "The New Kingdom." In *Ancient Egyptian Chronology*, edited by E. Hornung, R. Krauss, and D.A. Warburton, 197–217. Leiden: Brill.

Hornung, E., and E. Staehelin. 1974. *Studien zum Sedfest*. Geneva: Editions de Belles-Lettres.

Hovestreydt, W. 2014. "Sideshow or Not? On the Side-Rooms of the First Two Corridors in the Tomb of Ramesses III." In *The Workman's Progress: Studies in the Village of Deir el-Medina and other Documents from Western Thebes in Honour of Rob Demarée*, edited by B.J.J. Haring, O.E. Kaper, and R. van Walsem, 103–32. Leiden: Nederlands Instituut voor het Nabije Oosten.

Ikram, S. 2017. "From Thebes to Cairo: The Journey, Study, and Display of Egypt's Royal Mummies, Past, Present and Future." In *Volume in onore di M. Capasso*, edited by P. Davoli, 867–83. Lecce: University of Lecce.

James, P. 1991. *Centuries of Darkness: A Challenge to the Conventional Chronology of Old World Archaeology*. London: Jonathan Cape.

———. 2017. "The Levantine War-Records of Ramesses III: Changing Attitudes, Past, Present and Future." *Antiguo Oriente* 15: 57–148.

James, P., and P.G. van der Veen, eds. 2015. *Solomon and Shishak: Current Perspectives from Archaeology, Epigraphy, History and Chronology*. Oxford: Archaeopress.

Janssen, J.J. 1975. *Commodity Prices from the Ramessid Period: An Economic Study of the Village of Necropolis Workmen at Thebes*. Leiden: Brill.

———. 1979. "Background Information on the Strikes of Year 29 of Ramses III." *Oriens Antiquus* 18: 301–308.

Johnson, W.R. 2010. "The 'Temple of Millions of Years' of Ramesses III: The Publication Program of the Epigraphic Survey, Oriental Institute, University of Chicago (Chicago House) at Medinet Habu." In *Les temples de millions d'années et le pouvoir royal à Thèbes au Nouvel Empire: sciences et nouvelles technologies appliquées à l'archéologie*, edited by C. Leblanc and G. Zaki, 257–64. Cairo: Dar el-Kutub.

Jomard, E.F., ed. 1809–28. *Description de l'Égypte, ou, Recueil des observations et des recherches qui ont été faites en Égypte pendant l'expédition de l'armée française*. Paris: Imprimerie impériale.

Kahn, D. 2010. "Who Is Meddling in Egypt's Affairs? The Identity of the Asiatics in the Elephantine Stele of Sethnakhte and the Historicity of the Medinet Habu Asiatic War Reliefs." *JAEI* 2/1: 14–23.

———. 2011. "The Campaign of Ramesses III against Philistia." *JAEI* 3/4: 1–11.

———. 2015. "The Campaign of Ramesses III against Philistia." In *Solomon and Shishak: Current Perspectives from Archaeology, Epigraphy, History and Chronology; Proceedings of the Third BICANE Colloquium held at Sidney Sussex College, Cambridge 26–27 March, 2011*, edited by P. James and P.G. van der Veen, 274–81. Oxford: Archaeopress.

————. 2016. "The Historical Background of a Topographical List of Ramesses III." In *Rich and Great: Studies in Honour of Anthony J. Spalinger on the Occasion of His 70th Feast of Thot*, edited by R. Landgráfová and J. Mynářová, 161–68. Prague: Charles University in Prague, Faculty of Arts.

————. 2018. "Ramesses III and the Northern Levant: A Reassessment of the Sources." In *The Ramesside Period in Egypt: Studies into Cultural and Historical Processes of the 19th and 20th Dynasties*, edited by S. Kubisch and U. Rummel, 175–88. Berlin/Boston: Walter de Gruyter.

Kanawati, N. 2003. *Conspiracies in the Egyptian Palace: Unis to Pepy I*. London: Routledge.

Kaniewski, D., E. Van Campo, K. Van Lerberghe, T. Boiy, K. Vansteenhuyse, G. Jans, K. Nys, H. Weiss, C. Morhange, T. Otto, and J. Bretschneider. 2011. "The Sea Peoples, from Cuneiform Tablets to Carbon Dating." *Plos ONE* 6/6. http://doi.org/10.1371/journal.pone.0020232.

Kemp, B.J. 1995. "Outlying Temples at Amarna." In *Amarna Reports* VI, edited by B.J. Kemp, 411–62. London: Egypt Exploration Society.

Kitchen, K.A. 1968–90. *Ramesside Inscriptions: Historical and Biographical*. 8 vols. Oxford: Blackwell.

————. 1982. "The Twentieth Dynasty Revisited." *JEA* 68: 116–25.

————. 1984. "Family Relationships of Ramesses IX and the Late Twentieth Dynasty." *SAK* 11: 127–34.

————. 1991. "Review Feature: Centuries of Darkness. Egyptian Chronology: Problem or Solution?" *CAJ* 1/2: 235–39.

————. 1993–2014. *Ramesside Inscriptions: Translated and Annotated. Translations*. Oxford: Blackwell.

————. 1999. *Ramesside Inscriptions: Translated and Annotated. Notes and Comments*, II. Oxford: Blackwell.

————. 2012. "Ramesses III and the Ramesside Period." In *Ramesses III: The Life and Times of Egypt's Last Hero*, edited by E.H. Cline and D. O'Connor, 1–26. Ann Arbor: University of Michigan Press.

Kruchten, J.-M. 1979. "Une révolte du vizir sous Ramsès III à Athribis?" *Annuaire de l'Institut de Philologie et d'Histoire Orientales et Slaves* 2: 39–51.

Lane, E.W. 2000. *Description of Egypt*. Edited by J. Thompson. Cairo: American University in Cairo Press.

Leahy, A., ed. 1990. *Libya and Egypt c 1300–750 BC*. London: SOAS Centre of Near and Middle East Studies/Society for Libyan Studies.

Leblanc, C. 1989. *Ta set neferou: une nécropole de Thebes-Ouest et son histoire*, I. Cairo: Nubar.

————. 2001. "La véritable identité de Pentaouret, le Prince 'Maudit.'" *RdE* 52: 151–71.

————. 2001–2002. "Une nouvelle analyse de la double théorie des princes du temple de Ramsès III, à Medinet Habou." *Memnonia* 12/13: 191–218.

Lefébure, E. 1885. "Remarques sur différentes questions historiques." *ZÄS* 23: 121–27.

————. 1886–89. *Les hypogées royaux de Thèbes, seconde division: Notices des hypogées*. 3 vols. Paris: Ernest Leroux.

Lepsius, C.R. 1849–59. *Denkmaeler aus Aegypten und Aethiopien*. 12 vols. Berlin: Nicolaische Buchhandlung.

————. 1897–1913. *Denkmäler aus Aegypten und Aethiopien: Text*. 5 vols. Leipzig: J.C. Hinrichs.

Lesko, L.H. 1980. "The Wars of Ramses III." *Serapis* 6: 83–86.

————. 1992. "Egypt in the Twelfth Century B.C." In *The Crisis Years: The 12th Century B.C. from beyond the Danube to the Tigris*, edited by M.S. Joukowski and W.A. Ward, 151–56. Dubuque, IA: Kendall/Hunt Publishing.

Loffet, H., and V. Matoïan. 1996. "Le papyrus de Varzy." *RdÉ* 47: 29–36.

Malinine, M., G. Posener, and J. Vercoutter. 1968. *Catalogue des stèles du Serapéum de Memphis*, I. Paris: Éditions des musées nationaux.

Manassa, C. 2003. *The Great Karnak Inscription of Merneptah: Grand Strategy in the 13th Century B.C.* New Haven, CT: Yale Egyptological Seminar.

Manley, D., and P. Rée. 2001. *Henry Salt: Artist, Traveller, Diplomat, Egyptologist.* London: Libri.

Marciniak, M. 1982. "Réparations anciennes dans le tombeau de Ramsès III (no. 11) dans la Vallée des Rois." *Africana Bulletin* 31: 37–43.

———. 1983. "Deux campagnes épigraphiques au tombeau de Ramsès III dans la Vallée des Rois (no 11)." *Études et Travaux* 12: 295–305.

Mariette, A. 1880. *Abydos: description des fouilles exécutées sur l'emplacement de cette ville*, II. Paris: A. Franck/Imprimerie nationale.

Maspero, G. 1889. "Les Momies royales de Déir el-Baharî." In *Mémoires publiés par les membres de la Mission archéologique française au Caire* 1/4: 511–788. Paris: Ernest Leroux.

Mauric-Barberio, F. 2003. "Copie de textes à l'envers dans les tombes royales." In *Deir el-Médineh et la Vallée des Rois*, edited by G. Andreu, 173–94. Paris: Khéops.

———. 2004. "Reconstitution du décor de la tombe de Ramsès III (partie inférieure) d'après les manuscrits de Robert Hay." *BIFAO* 104: 389–456.

McClain, J.B., and W.R. Johnson. 2013. "A Fragment from the Reign of Tausret Reused at Medinet Habu." *JARCE* 49: 177–86.

McClain, J.B., J.L. Kimpton, K. Alberts, K. Vértes, and W.R. Johnson. 2011. "Preliminary Report on the Work of the Epigraphic Survey in the Temple of Khonsu at Karnak, 2009–2010." *JARCE* 47: 159–79.

Meeks, D. 2003. "Locating Punt." In *Mysterious Lands*, edited by D. O'Connor and S. Quirke, 53–58. London: UCL Press.

Mojsov, B. 1991–92. "A Royal Sarcophagus Reattributed." *BES* 11: 47–55.

Molleson, T., and M. Cox. 1993. *The Spitalfields Project*, II: *The Anthropology. The Middling Sort.* York: Council for British Archaeology.

Monnet, J. 1963. "Remarques sur la famille et les successeurs de Ramsès III." *BIFAO* 63: 209–36.

Montet, P. 1947. *La nécropole royale de Tanis* I: *Les constructions et le tombeau de Osorkon II à Tanis.* Paris: n.p.

Moran, W.L. 1992. *The Amarna Letters.* Baltimore and London: Johns Hopkins University Press.

Mountjoy, P.A. 1999. "Troia VII Reconsidered." *Studia Troia* 9: 295–346.

———. 2006. "Mykenische Keramik in Troia— ein Überblick." In *Troia: Archäologie eines Siedlungshügels und seiner Landschaft*, edited by M.O. Korfman, 241–52. Mainz: Philipp von Zabern.

Murnane, W.J. 1980. *United with Eternity: A Concise Guide to the Monuments of Medinet Habu.* Chicago: Oriental Institute/Cairo: American University in Cairo Press.

Nelson, H.H., and U. Hoelscher. 1929. *Medinet Habu—1924–28.* Chicago: University of Chicago Press.

Peden, A.J. 1994. *The Reign of Ramesses IV.* Warminster: Aris & Phillips.

Peet, T.E. 1930. *The Great Tomb-robberies of the Twentieth Egyptian Dynasty.* 2 vols. Oxford: Clarendon Press.

Piacentini, P., and C. Orsenigo. 2004. *La Valle dei Re Riscoperta: I giornali di scavo di Victor Loret (1898–1899) e altri inediti.* Milan: Skira/Università degli Studi di Milano.

Pococke, R. 1743. *A Description of the East, and Some Other Countries*, I: *Observations on Egypt.* London: the author.

Porter, B., and R.L.B. Moss. 1952. *Topographical Bibliography of Ancient Egyptian Hieroglyphic Texts, Reliefs and Paintings*, VII: *Nubia, Deserts, and Outside Egypt*. Oxford: Clarendon Press/Griffith Institute.

———. 1960–64. *Topographical Bibliography of Ancient Egyptian Hieroglyphic Texts, Reliefs and Paintings*, I: *The Theban Necropolis*. 2nd ed. Oxford: Clarendon Press/Griffith Institute.

———. 1972. *Topographical Bibliography of Ancient Egyptian Hieroglyphic Texts, Reliefs and Paintings*, II: *Theban Temples*. 2nd ed. Oxford: Griffith Institute.

Prisse d'Avennes, E. 1878–79. *Histoire de l'art égyptien d'après les monuments depuis les temps les plus reculés jusqu'à la domination romaine*. 3 vols. Paris: Arthus Bertrand.

Redford, D.B. 2018. *The Medinet Habu Records of the Foreign Wars of Ramesses III*. Leiden and Boston: Brill.

Redford, S. 2002. *The Harem Conspiracy: The Murder of Ramesses III*. De Kalb: Northern Illinois University Press.

Reeve, J., and M. Adams. 1993. *The Spitalfields Project*, I: *The Archaeology. Across the Styx*. York: Council for British Archaeology.

Reeves, C.N. 1990. *Valley of the Kings: The Decline of a Royal Necropolis*. London: Kegan Paul International.

Renouf, P. Le P. 1876. "Abstract of Criminal Proceedings in a Case of Conspiracy in the Time of Rameses III." *Records of the Past* 8: 53–65. London: Society for Biblical Archaeology.

Roberson, J.A. 2018. *Ramesside Inscriptions: Historical and Biographical*, IX. Liverpool: Abercromby Press.

Robins, G. 1981. "The Value of the Estimated Ages of the Royal Mummies at Death as Historical Evidence." *GM* 45: 63–68.

Rohl, D. 1995. *A Test of Time: The Bible—from Myth to History*. London: Century.

Rosellini, I. 1832–44. *I monumenti dell'Egitto e della Nubia: disegnati dalla Spedizione Scientifico-Letteraria Toscana in Egitto*. 12 vols. Pisa: Nicoló Capurro.

Sagrillo, T.L. 2015. "Shoshenq I and Biblical Šîšaq: A Philological Defense of Their Traditional Equation." In *Solomon and Shishak: Current Perspectives from Archaeology, Epigraphy, History and Chronology*, edited by P. James and P.G. van der Veen, 61–81. Oxford: Archaeopress.

Saleh, M., and H. Sourouzian. 1987. *The Egyptian Museum Cairo: Official Catalogue*. Mainz: Philipp von Zabern.

Säve-Söderbergh, T. 1941. *Ägypten und Nubien*. Lund: Ohlsson.

Schiaparelli, E. 1924. *Relazione sui lavori della Missione archeologica italiana in Egitto, anni 1903–1920*, I: *Esplorazione della "Valle delle Regine" nella necropoli di Tebe*. Turin: R. Museo di antichità.

Schott, S. 1953. *Das schöne Fest vom Wüstentale: Festbräuche einer Totenstadt*. Mainz: Steiner.

Schulman, A. 1960. "A Faience Stela from the New Kingdom." *Expedition* 2/4: 32–33.

Seele, K.C. 1955. "Some Remarks on the Family of Ramesses III." In *Ägyptologische Studien*, edited by O. Firchow, 296–314. Berlin: Akademie-Verlag.

Simons, J. 1937. *Handbook for the Study of Egyptian Topographical Lists Relating to Western Asia*. Leiden: Brill.

Smith, G.E. 1912. *The Royal Mummies*. Cairo: Institut français d'archéologie orientale.

Smith, H.S. 1976. *The Fortress of Buhen: The Inscriptions*. London: Egypt Exploration Society.

Snape, S. 2003. "The Emergence of Libya on the Horizon of Egypt." In *Mysterious Lands*, edited by D. O'Connor and S. Quirke, 93–106. London: UCL Press.

Somaglino, C., and P. Tallet. 2011. "Une mystérieuse route sud-orientale sous le règne de Ramsès III." *BIFAO* 111: 361–69.

———. 2013. "A Road to the Arabian Peninsula in the Reign of Ramesses III." In *Desert Road*

Archaeology in Ancient Egypt and Beyond, edited by F. Förster and H. Riemer, 511–18. Cologne: Institut für Ur- und Frühgeschichte der Universität zu Köln.

Strobel, K. 2011. "The Crucial 12th Century BC: The 'Fall of Empires' Revisited." In *Empires after the Empire: Anatolia, Syria and Assyria after Suppiluliuma II (ca. 1200–800/700 B.C.)*, edited by K. Strobel, 167–254. Florence: LoGisma editore.

Thomas, E. 1966. *The Royal Necropoleis of Thebes*, I: *The Major Cemeteries*. Princeton, NJ: Privately Printed.

Thompson, J. 2015. *Wonderful Things: A History of Egyptology*, I. Cairo: American University in Cairo Press.

Valbelle, D. 1985. *"Les ouvriers de la tombe": Deir el-Médineh à l'époque ramesside*. Cairo: Institut français d'archéologie orientale.

Vandersleyen, C. 1985. "Le dossier égyptien des Philistins." In *The Land of Israel: Cross-roads of Civilizations. Proceedings of the Conference Held in Brussels from the 3rd to the 5th of December 1984 to Mark the Twenty-fifth Anniversary of the Institute of Archaeology Queen Elisabeth of Belgium at the Hebrew University of Jerusalem, in Memory of Prof. Y. Yadin and Prof. Ch. Perelman*, edited by E. Lipiński, 39–54. Louvain: Peeters Publishers.

Ventura, R. 1986. *Living in a City of the Dead: A Selection of Topographical and Administrative Terms in the Documents of the Theban Necropolis*. Freiburg: Universitätsverlag/ Göttingen: Vandenhoeck & Ruprecht.

Vernier, É. 1927. *Bijoux et orfèvreries*. 2 vols. Cairo: Institut français d'archéologie orientale.

Vernus, P. 2003. *Affairs and Scandals in Ancient Egypt*. Translated by D. Lorton. Ithaca, NY: Cornell University Press.

von Beckerath, J. 1994. *Chronologie des ägyptischen Neuen Reiches*. Hildesheim: Gerstenberg.

———. 1999. *Handbuch der ägyptischen Königsnamen*. Mainz: Philipp von Zabern.

Weber, A. 2018. "First Report on the Publication and Conservation of the Tomb of Ramesses III in the Valley of the Kings (KV 11)." *JEA* 104: 59–69.

Weeks, K.R., ed. 2000. *Atlas of the Valley of the Kings*. Cairo: American University in Cairo Press.

———. 2001. *The Treasures of the Valley of the Kings: Tombs and Temples of the Theban West Bank in Luxor*. Cairo: American University in Cairo Press.

Weinstein, J. 1992. "The Collapse of the Egyptian Empire in the Southern Levant." In *The Crisis Years: The 12th century BC from beyond the Danube to the Tigris*, edited by M.S. Joukowski and W.A. Ward, 142–50. Dubuque, IA: Kendall/Hunt Publishing.

Wente, E.F. 1973. "A Prince's Tomb in the Valley of the Kings." *JNES* 32: 223–34.

Wilfong, T.G. 2002. *Women of Jeme: Lives in a Coptic Town in Late Antique Egypt*. Ann Arbor: University of Michigan Press.

Wilkinson, J.G. 1828–30. *Materia hieroglyphica*. 2 vols. Malta: Government Press.

———. 1835. *Topography of Thebes, and General View of Egypt*. London: John Murray.

———. 1837. *Manners and Customs of the Ancient Egyptians*. 3 vols. London: John Murray.

Wilkinson, R.H. 1995. "Symbolic Orientation and Alignment in New Kingdom Royal Tombs." In *Valley of the Sun Kings: New Explorations in the Tombs of the Pharaohs*, edited by R.H. Wilkinson, 74–81. Tucson: University of Arizona Egyptian Expedition.

Wilkinson, R.H., ed. 2011. *The Temple of Tausret: The University of Arizona Egyptian Expedition Tausret Temple Project, 2004–2011*. Tucson: University of Arizona Egyptian Expedition.

Wilson, P. 2002. "Rameses III, Giovanni Belzoni and the Mysterious Reverend Browne." In *Egypt through the Eyes of Travellers*, edited by P. Starkey and Nadia El Kholy, 45–56. Durham: ASTENE.

SOURCES OF IMAGES

All images by the author, except as listed below:

1. Dyan Hilton.
2. Mariette 1880: pl. 52.
4. © Trustees of the British Museum.
5. Centre Franco-Egyptien d'Etude des Temples de Karnak.
7. Weeks 2000.
9. Martin Davies.
13, top. Francis Dzikowski, © and courtesy Theban Mapping Project (13546).
13, bottom. Martin Davies.
16, top. Dylan Bickerstaffe.
16, bottom. Gerry Allaby, courtesy Egypt Exploration Society.
24. Martin Davies.
34. Epigraphic Survey 1930: pl. 19.
35. Adapted from Epigraphic Survey 1930: fig. 2.
37. Epigraphic Survey 1930: pl. 32.
38, bottom. Epigraphic Survey 1930: pl. 37.
40. Epigraphic Survey 1932: pl. 72.
41. Epigraphic Survey 1932: pl. 88.
42. Author's collection.
43. Epigraphic Survey 1930: pl. 9.
44. Salima Ikram.
44, inset. Gardiner and Peet 1917: pl. lxxiii[273].
46, left. © Trustees of the British Museum.
46, right. H.S. Smith 1976: pl. xxv[1]
51. Dyan Hilton.
54, left. Lepsius 1849–59: III, pl. 207g.

60. Martin Davies.

68. Pierpoint Morgan Library.

69. Dyan Hilton.

70. Epigraphic Survey 1970: pl. 646.

71. © Trustees of the British Museum.

73. Martin Davies.

78. Dyan Hilton.

84, bottom. Martin Davies.

86. Dyan Hilton.

94. Adapted from Weeks 2000.

96. Martin Davies.

104. Dyan Hilton.

105. Dylan Bickerstaffe.

106. Florence Barberio.

107. Champollion 1844–89: I, 422–23.

108a–b. Lefébure 1886–89: II, pl. 58.

108c. Lefébure 1886–89: II, pl. 61.

109. Lefébure 1886–89: II, pl. 64.

110, left. Leslie D. Black.

110, right. David Robbins.

111. Dyan Hilton.

112. Salima Ikram.

113d. © Trustees of the British Museum.

115. Maspero 1889: 564, fig. 19.

117. Author's collection.

118. Félix Teynard.

119. Wikimedia Commons.

120. Pococke 1743: pl. xxx.

121. Pococke 1743: pl. xxxii.

122. U.S. Library of Medicine.

123a. Bruce 1790: pl. oppo. p. 129

123a, inset. Martin Davies.

123b. Jomard 1809–28: Ant. II, pl 91.

124. © The Fitzwilliam Museum, Cambridge.

125. British Library.

126. British Library.

127. Salima Ikram collection.

128a. Daressy 1909: pl. xx.

128b–c. Maspero 1889: pl. xvii.

128d. G.E. Smith 1912: pl. l.

129. Vernier 1927: pl. iv, v.

130. Benédite 1894: pl. I, v, vi.

131. Photoglob, via Library of Congress.

INDEX

The names of ancient Egyptian kings are CAPITALIZED.